Divorced &
Still Highly Favored

Divorced &
STILL HIGHLY FAVORED

Janice R. Love
Foreword by Ondrea L. Davis

Divorced and Still Highly Favored. Copyright © 2015 by Janice R. Love. All rights reserved. No part of this book may be used or reproduced by any means without written permission from the author with the exception of brief quotations in printed reviews.

Published by Divine Garden Press, LLC
P.O. Box 371
Soperton, GA 30457
www.divinegardenpress.com

ISBN-13: 978-0692404157
ISBN-10: 0692404155
Library of Congress Control Number: 2015935913

Scripture taken from the Holy Bible, King James Version. Copyright © 1990 by Thomas Nelson, Incl. All rights reserved.

Scripture taken from the New King James Version®. Copyright © 1982 by Thomas Nelson. Used by permission. All rights reserved.

Scripture taken from Contemporary English Version®. Copyright © 1995 American Bible Society. All rights reserved.

Scripture taken from the Common English Bible®, CEB Copyright © 2010, 2011 by Common English Bible™. Used by permission. All rights reserved worldwide.

Scripture taken from the The ESV® Bible (The Holy Bible, English Standard Version®) copyright © 2001 by Crossway, a publishing ministry of Good News Publishers. ESV® Text Edition: 2011

Scripture taken from the HOLY BIBLE, NEW INTERNATIONAL VERSION®, Copyright © 1973, 1978, 1984 by International Bible Society. Used by permission of Zondervan Publishing House. All rights reserved.

Scripture taken from The Living Bible copyright © 1971 by Tyndale House Foundation. Used by permission of Tyndale House Publishers Inc., Carol Stream, Illinois 60188. All rights reserved.

Scripture taken from the Message. Copyright © 1993, 1994, 1995, 1996, 2000, 2001, 2002. Used by permission of NavPress Publishing Group.

Scripture taken from Holy Bible, New Living Translation copyright © 1996, 2004, 2007, 2013 by Tyndale House Foundation. Used by permission of Tyndale House Publishers Inc., Carol Stream, Illinois 60188. All rights reserved.

Scripture quotations taken from the New American Standard Bible®, Copyright © 1960, 1962, 1963, 1968, 1971, 1972, 1973, 1975, 1977, 1995 by The Lockman Foundation used by permission.

Cover Design & Interior Layout by Divine Lit Services
www.divinelit.com

Author Photo © Worth a 1000 Words Studios

To my Mother, the late Helen Pocahontas Briddell Emerson who loved me unconditionally, regardless of who I was married to. Thank you for the example you set for me while you were here on earth. Your presence is with me always.

Table of Contents

FOREWORD	i
INTRODUCTION	v

BEFORE DIVORCE: IS DIVORCE YOUR FINAL ANSWER?

1.	Let's Stay Together	1
2.	Have You Tried Everything?	8
3.	Intercession, Intervention, or Interference?	14
4.	Christians Get Divorced?	22
5.	What the Bible Really Says About Divorce	28
6.	Is Divorce a Sin?	34
7.	It May Not Be About You	40
8.	Whose Fault Is It?	44
9.	Failed at Marriage More Than Once?	49
10.	Separation	56

DURING DIVORCE: THE GOOD, THE BAD, AND THE UGLY

11.	Timing	65
12.	Divorce is a Life Stressor	71
13.	A Thin Line Between Love and Hate	76
14.	The Rumor Mill	81
15.	Divorce and Depression	87
16.	Change is Inevitable	94
17.	Friend Custody	102
18.	Letting Others Down	108
19.	Loneliness	115
20.	Money, Money, Money	120
21.	Outrage and Anger	129
22.	Resentment	135
23.	Worried about the Future	141
24.	Self-Esteem	146

25. Regret 152

After Divorce: The Catalyst for a Highly Favored Life

26. Happy Anniversary 159
27. Embarrassed to Say Divorced? 163
28. Is it Okay for Me to Be Happy? 167
29. Gratitude 171
30. Self-Reflection 176
31. Lead Us Not Into Temptation 182
32. Forgiveness 188
33. Don't Stop Praying 195
34. You are a Survivor 200
35. Take Care of Yourself 205
36. Be a Blessing 212
37. Single and Satisfied 217
38. Moving On 222
39. Love and Remarriage 227
40. Still Highly Favored 236

Conclusion 237

Acknowledgements 241

Resources and References 243

Foreword

What comes to mind when you hear the word divorce? Some responses may include concern for the children, the wife having to step up as head of the household or maybe even the grief over loss of a relationship. Now more specifically, what thoughts surface when this divorce involves two Christians? The most prevalent responses relate to sin, in the form of disobedience to God, as well as public shame and guilt. What I have come to realize is that all things, even the most debilitating situations, can work together for good if we allow them to.

Unfortunately, even members of the Kingdom of God sometime fall into the same trap that those in the world have been ensnared by. We have likened ourselves unto those who have no hope that God can and will restore our marriages. The faith and joy that we began with on our journey with our spouse may have wavered along the way. Per biblical teaching, we are aware that God is not pleased with divorce, yet the Church experiences this very challenge at an alarmingly high rate. With such an epidemic, the real question has become, *How can we effectively combat the enemy that constantly seeks to steal, kill, and destroy our families?* Be this known unto us, it is certainly not in our best interest to hand over our loved ones to the enemy of our souls. We must stand up with confidence and take our position in the good fight of faith.

As a divorcee, I understand the pain of realizing that the vows you declared before God will be terminated. You feel as if you have failed yourself, others round you, and most importantly, God. One thing I know now that I did not know then is that God still favors me. This is not because I want Him to overlook my mistakes; it is simply because He loves me and knows the desires and intent of my heart. One of those desires being the preservation of our legacy within the Church. I do not wish any family to suffer the consequences of a divorce as my own has. Nor will I rest on the sidelines while the enemy continues to attack us with such ferocity.

As a result of my experience, I believe even more in the sanctity of marriage. I am adamant about the fact that God did not institute marriage and the family structure to be doomed and despondent. Husbands, wives, and children were not meant to be depressed and defeated. No indeed! Jesus came that we might have life more abundantly! Therefore, we must be transformed by the renewing of our minds in order to graduate from thinking beneath our privilege to that of emotional prosperity. Because of His sacrifice for us, we must also sacrifice to maintain this abundance. Herein lies the battle between our spirit man and our own flesh.

Each week, an astounding number of men, women, and children attend Sunday worship services and Bible classes as their hearts bleed in our pews. Yet we do not acknowledge their pain. From the pulpit to the door, we must realize that the pressures and ordeals that the Christian family experiences are ultimately orchestrated to abolish effective ministry. If we cannot salvage our own marriages and maintain healthy families, how can we help the lost souls who require the example of Jesus' attributes? The key is in us acknowledging that this is not just a natural battle. This is spiritual warfare!

The foundation of every war, regardless of which side you are on, is strategy. Research and planning paired with proper offense and defense tactics are components of any successful strategy. We must utilize these same components to fortify the family structure by promoting emotional and spiritual health in our homes so that the gates of hell do not prevail against us. This includes, but is not limited to, being assertive enough to address taboo issues, establishing programs within our local churches to teach from a godly perspective, and partnering with Christian counselors, when we as leaders are not equipped to handle certain issues, when necessary. Let us not continue to perish due to lack of knowledge. Instead, we should arm ourselves by implementing any and all measures and tools that will promote the healing and restoration of families; we can be victorious in all things. This type of process requires not only discussion, but it solicits action.

One piece of advice I continuously share with my three children is that you don't always have to personally experience life's disappointments and heartbreak; you can learn from the choices of others. Lady Janice Love was inspired by God to address the Christian divorce epidemic with this book. Who better to help others with this challenging subject matter than one who has walked both side of this fence? *Divorced & Still Highly Favored* is an effective tool that enables singles, and married alike, to glean from her personal experiences in order to avoid landmines that the enemy has planted to annihilate God's perfect plan for the family structure.

We cannot forget that this plan of abundance does not always refer to physical riches, but also our mentality. According to Ephesians 3:20, we know that God, *"is able to do exceeding abundantly, above all we can ask or think, according to the power that worketh in us..."* As Christians, we should accept the gift of abundant life that was destined for us by allowing God's power to work on our behalf in all aspects of our lives. He will not force Himself on any of us.

In lieu of our free will, we must choose to activate the power He has given us access to and take our families back by force. Remember that no matter how badly our marriages have deteriorated, God is able to resurrect the relationships that show no signs of life and have already begun to stink so that His glory is revealed. As a matter of fact, God takes pleasure in performing miracles because it is His will that we be healed from the inside out.

Thinking and walking in God's abundance will require effort on our part. On some days, there will be simple paths to walk and on others, mountains to climb. In either case, the objective is to fight with all our might to fortify Christian households. When our might runs out, the strength of the Lord carries us to the finishing point. The wisdom poured into this book will aid in the everyday battles that present themselves as we navigate the paths to abundant living as strong family units.

My prayer is that by reading Janice's testimony and taking heed to her words of experience, we will end the last page empowered to seek God for direction, utilize honesty regarding our own shortcomings, and extend mercy to others when we feel we have been failed. The souls of others are depending on Christians to represent The Light in such a dark and dreary world. So let us acknowledge the magnitude of this spiritual war and equip ourselves to stand until we have obtained complete victory over the enemy of our families!

Ondrea L. Davis

Award-Winning Author of *How Could My Husband Be Gay?*

Introduction

This is my life's work; helping people understand and respond to this message. It came as a sheer gift to me, a real surprise; God handling all the details. I was the least qualified of any available Christians. God saw to it that I was equipped, but you can be sure it had nothing to do with my natural abilities. And so here I am, preaching and writing about things that are way over my head, the inexhaustible riches and generosity of Christ.
Ephesians 3: 7-11 (MSG)

According to the high school memory book I completed my senior year, I was supposed to go to medical school, become a psychiatrist, and marry a guy named Gerald. We were going to be the parents of two boys, own a big house, possess two cars, and live happily ever after in a nice neighborhood on the east coast. In my vision, Gerald's occupation wasn't important because as a psychiatrist I was going to make a lot of money.

Life actually turned out quite differently than I expected. I didn't go to medical school; instead, I earned a Master's degree in Biological Psychology and returned to Oklahoma. Gerald's name turned out to be Richard and we married after I finished graduate school. Richard was just starting out in the ministry and felt like he needed to be married as soon as possible. I had just finished graduate school and was ready for the next phase in my life. We married after dating for five months and believed we were starting on the right track.

We became parents after being married for two years and gave birth to our first son. Life was good, but we struggled as a couple. When our son was in kindergarten, we separated and then divorced. The good news is we got back together two years later, remarried, and went on a honeymoon in Cancun, Mexico. We did not tell anyone what we were doing and when our family found out, they were delighted that we were back together. We were pretty sure we knew what went wrong the first time and would now live happily ever after the second time around. A new house and a beautiful baby girl added to our bliss.

A year after our daughter was born, we resumed some of the same problems, arguments, and marital discord. Five years into the remarriage, we relocated from Oklahoma City to the Kansas City area. The move, as well as my husband's new job as the pastor of a growing church congregation, was exciting. Life appeared fabulous on the outside as we worked together for the sake of the church. However, appearances were deceiving as we were unhappy in our home. I began to focus more on my job and the children, while he focused on the church. We grew further and further apart, remaining together for the sake of the church and our children. In year six, I decided I no longer wanted to live a lie before God and asked to be released from the marriage. Six months later, on Valentine's Day, our second divorce was final. Four years later, I married another pastor with six children and we became a stepfamily of ten people. Wow! Life, love, and marriage were really much different than I envisioned, so much so that I wrote a survival guide for stepmoms entitled *One Plus One Equals Ten: A First Lady's Guide for Stepmoms*.

I was in the middle of writing my first book when the Lord revealed to me I was to also write a book about divorce. After all, I went through a divorce first before I ended up with stepfamily issues. Oh, how quickly I had forgotten. Before being a part of a stepfamily I had, by the grace of God, survived divorce, single parenting, and dating with children. At first, the recommendation to write about my divorce experiences didn't make sense to me. I didn't want to focus on a time in my life where I had been at my lowest. I was now happily married to the love of my life and our ministry focus was helping blended families, so why would I want to write a book about divorce?

One summer morning, I was driving my 27 mile, one-way commute to work, when a thought appeared very strongly in my mind. The thought was simply, *You have another book to write.* I looked around and said to myself, "Where did that come from?" I then realized the Holy Spirit had planted the thought because the same thought came again as a whisper. "You have another book to write when you finish this one, and you are to focus on divorce." Before leaving the house for work, I had read an article in the Kansas City Star entitled "Camilla's Decision a Relief." The gist of the story was Prince Charles' wife, Camilla, had made the decision not to attend the ten year anniversary memorial service for Princess Diana. Even though I was a diehard Princess Diana fan, my heart went out to Camilla because I understood her decision. I don't know why I felt the need to pray for Camilla, but I did, praying for her strength. I knew she was going to be criticized for her decision, but it didn't matter; either way it was going to be a difficult day for her. I understood what it was like to be the second wife of a prominent man in the community whose former wife had died.

A few moments later, my thoughts returned to Princess Diana. I remember being home from college the summer of her fairytale wedding. Along with my youngest sister, Gregorita, we got up early in the morning to watch the televised wedding of the century. I smiled thinking about how excited we were, when I suddenly remembered that their fairytale wedding had sadly ended in divorce. I began to imagine what Diana's life must have been like after she divorced Prince Charles. The thoughts remained in the forefront of my mind the rest of my workday.

After arriving home, I searched the internet for books and articles written about Diana after the divorce from Prince Charles. Based on what I had gone through, I could only imagine what she experienced emotionally. Diana was noted for her sense of style, charisma, humor, and high-profile charity work, yet her philanthropic endeavors were overshadowed by her difficult marriage to Prince Charles. I searched for pictures of her on the internet taken after the divorce. I looked carefully at the pictures and didn't see pain in her eyes. What I saw was a confident woman who had experienced a very public divorce, however, had made every effort to move on with her life. She knew who she was with or without being the wife of Prince Charles.

I am in no way trying to compare myself to Princess Diana, but I too had made the decision to divorce a man who held a prominent position in society. My ex-husband was not headed towards being a king, but he held a prominent position in the Christian and public sector, that of pastor of a Baptist church. Because he was a pastor, a private divorce was out of the question. This not only was it our family's issue, but the issue of the church and the community. Our entire church, including individual families were deeply affected by our decision to divorce. This left me feeling sorry for the church and for all of the couples and children who had wanted to pattern their lives after ours. After all, we had appeared to be the perfect couple.

So one would ask, why should I write a book about Christian divorce, and what would make me the expert?

Besides, Christians shouldn't divorce, right? Despite what Christians should and shouldn't do, divorce has occurred twice in my life, even though it was with the same husband. Who ever heard of marrying and divorcing the same man twice? I know Elizabeth Taylor and Richard Burton married and divorced twice, but I thought those kinds of things only happened in Hollywood. Somehow, Richard and I couldn't make it past seven years. For us, seven seemed to be an unlucky number.

Allow me to jump ahead and let you know that both my ex-husband and I have gone on to marry wonderful people and are both extremely blessed in our current marriages. I am grateful for him and his wife, and I wish them the best. The most wonderful blessing is that we all get along. We have created an environment in which the children we brought into this world can depend on us to respect each other and to protect them as much as possible from the potential harmful effects of divorce. I felt like I needed to say that because what you will not find in this book is any attempt to point fingers or criticize my ex-husband. "Let no corrupt communication proceed out of your mouth, but that which is good to the use of edifying, that it may minister grace unto the hearers" (Ephesians 4:29 KJV).

Perhaps you are still married and pondering whether or not you should divorce. Let me be the first to encourage you to prayerfully consider your decision and seek help from a Christian counselor. If there is any way possible you can stay married, I would encourage you to do so. Seek help so you do not have to go down this devastating road. Working through marital issues may seem easy for me to say; I survived divorce twice. Like Princess Diana, my pictures may not show it, but it was one of the most difficult times in my life, and I would prefer that not even my worst enemies experience the death of a marital union.

This book is my story on how a God of love extended grace, mercy, and comfort to me when I needed it most. I want you to learn that nothing is too hard for God. Three vastly different sections describe my experiences before, during, and after divorce. Because I divorced the same man twice at different stages in my life, I will identify which divorce I am referring to by labeling them as divorce one and divorce two. By reading my experiences, I pray that you too can experience God's grace even while going through divorce. At the end of each chapter, I have included helpful scriptures to pray and meditate on. I hope you will find these scriptures to be helpful and comforting.

I pray that this book will be a blessing to anyone, but particularly to Christian women. This book is designed with hope in mind, hope for blessings in the lives of Christian women worldwide who are experiencing or whom have experienced the devastating effects of divorce. There is hope for the future. After all, God reminds us in Jeremiah 29:11 that He has our best interest at heart for our future. His plans are for good and not for disaster, to give you a future and a hope.

"Grace be unto you, and peace, from God our Father, and from the Lord Jesus Christ" (1 Corinthians 1:3, KJV).

BEFORE DIVORCE
Is Divorce Your Final Answer?

CHAPTER 1
Let's Stay Together

Love is patient, love is kind...... It always protects, always trusts, always hopes, always perseveres.
1 Corinthians 13: 4, 7 (NIV)

DON'T DO IT

Let me be the first to tell you that if you don't have to go down this road, please don't. Divorce is equal to death. It comes with much heartache, suffering, crying, grief, frustration, anger, and sorrow. As I stated previously, I wouldn't wish it on my worst enemy. My heart aches anytime I hear a couple is separating, having massive problems, or contemplating divorce. I remember so well how difficult my life became. I would prefer that everyone I know and love could figure out the secret of how to do it right the first time.

If you are in the contemplative stage, you should do everything possible to make your marriage work. The situation may not be as bad as it seems. I know it's tough, but try not to focus on all the negativity going on in your marriage right now. Allow your mind to think back to the happier times you shared. Couples who have been together for a long time will tell you their marriage was challenging especially when their children were younger, but they stuck it out and as a result stayed together and now they are content with their marriages.

FOR BETTER OR WORSE

Think about the vows you made, for better or worse. Just because it is worse right now doesn't mean you should give up. What exactly is worse? Is worse compulsive lying or adultery? Is worse a severe financial situation such as bankruptcy or a major tax debt? Is worse major interference from in-laws, or in the case of a blended family, children from another mother? Define what worse is for you. One person's worse may be tolerable for another.

You may not really know what worse is until after the divorce. I was talking with a friend about life, marriage, and relationships and how to measure happiness on a scale of one to ten. If you place happiness on a scale of one to ten, with one being absolutely miserable and ten being ecstatically happy, most people who are considering divorce will rate their happiness at five or below. The bad news is the divorce process can take you down to a level of two or three. It may be a long road before you feel you are even a five.

WHAT IS THE PROBLEM IN YOUR MARRIAGE?

I have always believed that there are three major areas a married couple argue or disagree on. In no particular order they are: money, sex, and family. If there is more, many have a root in these three. A husband may spend a lot of time complaining about his wife's cooking, but the real issue may be he feels like they are not having sex often enough. Think about your situation. Do your problems stem from any of the following situations?

Money

Did you marry for money or financial reasons?
Are you experiencing financial problems as a family?
Do you have different spending and saving habits?
Is one spending too much or too little?
Is someone working too much?
Is someone not working enough or not at all?
Are there arguments related to church giving?
Are financial responsibilities being neglected?
Do you operate as separate entities financially?
Is there selfishness in giving to each other?
Is there anger and resentment related to money?

Sex

Does one person want sex more than the other?
Is your sex life non-existent?
Was the relationship based on physical or sexual attraction or lust?
Is someone having sex or a relationship outside of the marriage?
Is there a physical problem that causes problems related to sex?
Is there a sexual addiction related to computers or the internet?
Is there sexual abuse in one's past?
Do you bring other problems into the bedroom?
Is your sex life boring?
Is romance missing?
Do you find your spouse undesirable?
Is sex used for manipulation, power, or control?
Are there differences in attitude about sex, passion, and romance?

Is there anger and resentment related to sex?

Family

Are the in-laws creating problems in your marriage?
Do family members not approve of your marriage?
Does your spouse run to family with all of your problems?
Has the umbilical cord not been severed?
Do you disagree on having children or how many to have?
Are you unable to have children?
Does someone else run your household?
Do you disagree on how to raise the children?
Are you experiencing problems related to step-parenting?
Do you engage in family activities separately?
Do you spend time with one side of the family more than the other?
Do you love your children more than your spouse?
Are there cultural differences that cause disagreement?
Is there anger and resentment related to family members?

God knew we would have family problems which is why he talked about each person leaving their parents to be united as one. "For this reason a man shall leave [behind] his father and his mother and be joined to his wife and cleave closely to her permanently. And the two shall become one flesh, so that they are no longer two, but one flesh" (Mark 10:7-8 AMP).

Notice that the last question of each grouping asks if there's any anger or resentment related to the subject. Once anger and resentment are present, an unforgiving spirit can cloud one's thoughts and hopes. For example, I remember being angry at my ex-husband because he spent a large sum of money without my input. I started with disappointment because I felt like he had spent too much money, then I began to resent any money spent on his behalf. One thing led to another to the point I didn't want to discuss money at all. My anger over money led to hostility.

The last thing on my mind when I made the decision to get married was divorce. I had no reason to do a prenuptial agreement because we loved each other and planned to live happily ever after. We married and had a few ups and downs but divorce wasn't an option. I had so many hopes and dreams for our family. My husband grew up without his father so he never wanted to live apart from his children. Although his parents never married, mine had been married for over 40 years. My parents had stayed together through some very difficult circumstances, so we could do the same.

Perhaps you are just thinking about getting a divorce and haven't started the process yet. Can you trust God to fix your marriage? Jeremiah 32:27 states, "I am the Lord, the God of all mankind. Is anything too hard for me?" Remember, with God all things are possible. Therefore reconciliation is possible. Even if your marriage is in serious trouble and you feel like there is no love left, there is hope. Reconciliation means the re-establishing of cordial relations or getting two things or people to correspond.

Just because you have hired a lawyer and started drawing up divorce papers, you do not have to go through with the process. The judge may have already hit the gavel and pronounced your divorce as final. The ink may still be wet on the paper where you both signed. You may already be living apart and may have already changed your name back to your maiden name. Remember if you chose to reconcile it is never too late. Start slowly if you have to by going on a date with your spouse. Talk about the good times, admit your mistakes, visit a marriage counselor, and dedicate time for focused prayer and fasting. Ask God for His direction on what He wants you to do. Seek whatever professional help you need. Fight for your marriage. Spend the money if you need to because divorce is a lot more expensive.

Divorce can cost thousands of dollars. Relocation expenses, attorney fees, lost time at work, are only a drop in the bucket for the financial devastation divorce can have. Why not spend $700 on an intensive marriage counselor and try to make it work?

Helpful Scriptures

Don't refuse to meet each other's needs unless you both agree for a short period of time to devote yourselves to prayer. Then come back together again so that Satan might not tempt you because of your lack of self-control.
1 Corinthians 7: 5 (CEB)

If he came in single, he will leave single. If he came in married, then his wife will leave with him.
Exodus 21:3 (CEB)

For this reason a man shall leave [behind] his father and his mother and be joined to his wife and cleave closely to her permanently. And the two shall become one flesh, so that they are no longer two, but one flesh.
Mark 10:7-8 (AMP)

But Jesus beheld them, and said unto them, With men this is impossible; but with God all things are possible.
Matthew 19:26 (KJV)

If you love money and wealth, you will never be satisfied with what you have. This doesn't make sense either. The more you have, the more everyone expects from you. Your money won't do you any good--others will just spend it for you. Ecclesiastes 5:10-11 (CEV)

Have respect for marriage. Always be faithful to your partner, because God will punish anyone who is immoral or unfaithful in marriage. Hebrews 13:4 (CEV)

Chapter 2
Have You Tried Everything?

Jesus looked at them carefully and said, "It's impossible with human beings, but not with God. All things are possible for God." Mark 10: 27 (CEB)

I have to ask the question you really don't want me to ask. Have you and your spouse tried everything to make your marriage work? Before making it final, try one or all three of these options: counseling, prayer, and rekindling your marriage. I know you are saying to yourself, *Janice has a lot of nerve trying to convince me to stay in my broken marriage when she followed through with the divorce process not just once, but twice.* All I can say is that God works in mysterious ways and He has taken my mess and turned it into a message, and instructed me to try to convince others not to make the same mistakes I did.

COUNSELING

Have you tried counseling or coaching? There are some really good marriage counselors out there available to you. In our first divorce, we went to see our pastor instead of a professional marriage counselor. Warning, not all pastors are trained in marriage and family counseling. Yes, pastors and religious leaders have possibly worked with many couples and can pray with you, spend time listening to your issues, and perhaps make great recommendations;

however, if they are not professionally trained to handle marital issues, you may need to get a referral.

If you are employed and your employer provides an Employee Assistance Program (EAP), check to see what services are available to you and your spouse. Often you are able to receive services free of charge or for a minimal fee. Even if it does cost, your marriage is worth it. Remember, a divorce is a lot more expensive than three to five counseling sessions. The process will be more beneficial if the two of you attend sessions together. However, if your spouse will not attend counseling with you, go alone.

Sometimes the best marriage counselors in the world don't have a degree or training in marriage and family counseling. There are couples you know who have walked in your shoes and have been successful at marriage for many years. There are probably couples in your church whom you admire who are willing to sit down with you and your spouse and share their experiences. Numerous couples have survived infidelity, financial issues, child issues, and more and are happy to share with you. I have heard my mother-in-law talk about the difficult times in her marriage of sixty-nine years and how she wanted to give up on their marriage and walk away. She is thankful now that they stayed together.

Churches all across America have strong marriage ministries. Some of them you can access online. Check out Family Matters First managed by my friends Jim and Teresa Adams. Their marriage ministry has now spread to a weekly podcast (familymattersfirst.org) designed to help couples and families. Does your church have a marriage ministry? My current husband and I present annually at a variety of churches that offer marriage ministries, seminars, and retreats. Other churches celebrate marriages in unique ways by sponsoring couple retreats and other fun activities for married couples. If your church has a marriage ministry, you can network and share with other couples who may be going through similar challenges. Often marriage ministries will focus on biblical studies that are applicable for new couples or couples who need a spark in their marriage.

Prayer

If you are a Christian, I can't stress enough that you should be praying for direction before making a decision. What is your prayer life like? Are you praying regularly or every now and then? If you are praying, what exactly are you praying about? Are you praying that the Lord will deliver you from the marriage? Are you praying that your spouse will change? Are you praying that you will change?

Divorce is a decision that should not be made without prayer. Are you praying together as a couple? I have found it hard to be mad at my husband when we are praying together regularly. I also find it difficult to remain angry at him when I am praying for him. What is your experience with prayer as a couple? Do you pray together daily, weekly, or only during a crisis? Are you unequally yoked and don't pray together? Do you study the bible or attend a bible study together? Do you maintain family devotion? Over the years, I have found some excellent devotionals available for couples that can help you determine what you should be praying about in your marriage. *Night Light for Couples* by James and Shirley Dodson is an excellent resource available online or in a hardback. Lifeway.com has many resources and Bible studies for couples that can be done in the privacy of your home. Have you watched the movie *Fireproof* (based on the book *The Love Dare*) or read the book *Praying Through the Deeper Issues of Marriage* by Stormie Omartian?

Sadly, when I was sure I wanted to divorce, I refused to pray with my spouse except in corporate worship. I gave up on praying for the marriage to work out. We were praying separately asking for help to get out of the marriage and for grace related to all the bi-products of the divorce process. I was praying that he would be able to keep his church and for our house to sell at a profit. I was praying for our children and for my sanity. I want to encourage you to have prayer time as a couple. Prayer may be the only defense you have left.

Rekindle Your Marriage

Do you find yourself saying things like: "We have grown apart?" "We fell out of love with one another." "We don't enjoy one another anymore." "Our marriage has lost its spark." "We are like two ships passing in the night." "Now that our children are grown, we don't have anything in common anymore." I have heard these comments as many times as I have used them myself. If true love was there at one time, love can be rekindled.

After we divorced the first time, we remarried two years later. Once the bitterness, confusion, and anger subsided, we began to have crucial conversations about what went wrong the first time. After a while, we began going on a date occasionally and then more regularly, until we were seeing each other every day.

Think about the reasons you married in the first place. Reminisce on your love story. Play and listen to your favorite love song. Get away from it all and recreate your honeymoon or happier times. Practice forgiveness if you have been wronged and seek forgiveness in those areas you have offended your spouse. Hang out with other couples who have healthy marriages. Make a list of positive characteristics about your spouse. For every negative thought you have about your spouse, replace the thoughts with five positive ones. Most of all watch what you say about your spouse and your marriage. "Watch the way you talk. Let nothing foul or dirty come out of your mouth. Say only what helps, each word a gift" (Ephesians 4:29, MSG).

Helpful Scriptures

So wives submit to their husbands in everything like the church submits to Christ. As for husbands, love your wives just like Christ loved the church and gave himself for her. Ephesians 5:24-25 (CEB)

Submit to one another out of reverence for Christ. Wives, submit yourselves to your own husbands as you do to the Lord. For the husband is the head of the wife as Christ is the head of the church, his body, of which he is the Savior. Now as the church submits to Christ, so also wives should submit to their husbands in everything. Ephesians 5:21-24 (NIV)

Husbands, in the same way be considerate as you live with your wives, and treat them with respect as the weaker partner and as heirs with you of the gracious gift of life, so that nothing will hinder your prayers. 1 Peter 3:7 (NIV)

Marriage should be honored by all, and the marriage bed kept pure, for God will judge the adulterer and all the sexually immoral. Hebrews 13:4 (NIV)

From now on, brothers and sisters, if anything is excellent and if anything is admirable, focus your thoughts on these things: all that is true, all that is holy, all that is just, all that is pure, all that is lovely, and all that is worthy of praise. Philippians 4:8 (CEB)

Chapter 3
Intervention, Intercession, or Interference?

I urge you, first of all, to pray for all people. Ask God to help them; intercede on their behalf, and give thanks for them. 1 Timothy 2:1 (NLT)

INTERVENTION: a coming between.

INTERCESSION: an interposing or pleading on behalf of another person, a prayer to God on behalf of another.

INTERFERENCE: the act of hindering or obstructing or impeding.

When experiencing a divorce, one of the most difficult tasks you will encounter is informing friends, family, and fellow church members of your status. Because divorce is such a stressful time in one's life, you need all the support you can get, especially from your Christian friends and family. The first time I was divorced, I learned a valuable lesson: You can't talk to everybody. In fact, you have to seek guidance from God by praying about who to talk to, what to say, and when to say it.

Intervention

When we initially thought that we were headed for divorce one, we requested a counseling session with our pastor. Because my ex was the assistant pastor at the time, our pastor knew a lot about our history. He not only tried to intervene because he was our pastor, but because he loved and cared for both of us. Of course he strongly encouraged us to hang in there for the sake of our son and even shared some of his personal marital struggles. Upon his recommendation, we met with him a few more times in an attempt to resolve our issues. He prayed with us and suggested professional counseling if his intervention did not help. Although our pastor continued to pray for us, our plight did not improve. I believe our minds were made up. Our pastor remained supportive of both of us even after announcing we were headed for divorce court.

Outside of the pastor, is the church equipped to help couples in crisis? Actually, not all pastors are equipped to counsel couples in marital crisis. Some have gained credentials in marriage and family counseling, while others rely on spiritual guidance and experience working with other couples. I wonder if there are any statistics out there of whether or not pastoral counseling encourages the couples to stay together.

Perhaps participating in a marriage ministry would have helped us. In our church, the closest ministry would have been the young adult ministry which consisted of singles and other young married couples. Our group contained more singles than married couples. When members of our young adult group learned of our impending divorce, there was one individual that was concerned enough to attempt intervention with me. He wanted to encourage me that he and his wife were praying for us to get back together. There were no other couples who took an interest in our marriage or attempted to convince us to stay together. It may have helped the first time around to speak with a couple who had stuck it out and were glad they did.

In divorce two, counseling was out of the question. We were in a new area and did not know who we could trust. Even though secular counseling had not been helpful in the past, I considered going to a counselor through my work employee assistance program (EAP). My concern with the EAP counselors was their inability to truly grasp our concerns as a ministry couple. I wasn't aware of any Christian counselors in the area and was afraid to ask anyone for a recommendation. Besides, our minds were made up since we had gone through divorce before.

Intercession

When Christians experience difficulties in our lives, we often feel comfortable asking others to pray for us. We may not share all of the painful details, but will request special prayer from our friends, family, church members, and sometimes complete strangers. I have seen many Facebook requests from my on-line friends asking for prayer for one reason or another. Often I will silently whisper a prayer for them and write their names in my prayer journal. I was no different. When going through our divorce, I asked select individuals to pray for me, but never was specific as to what my needs were.

In divorce one, we were in our 20's and learned some valuable lessons. We both confided in some of our Christian peers. I confided in a girlfriend who was going through the same turmoil I was, that of a struggling marriage, headed towards divorce court. It had never been truer that "misery loves company." We stayed on the phone for hours complaining about our spouses and comparing whose marriage was worse. We supported one another and justified our actions to divorce and even promised to pray for one another. Soon, it was easy for our stories to become intertwined and distorted. Be careful that you do not buddy up with someone who encourages you to do the same thing they are doing.

During divorce two, I got several phone calls from church members, but I rarely answered the phone. Thank goodness for caller ID. One time the phone rang and I recognized it was a senior woman from our church. She called to offer her advice and to let me know she was praying for us. I admired and respected her and was willing to listen to her wisdom. Then she asked the question, "Why would you turn your back on your family?" I wasn't sure how to answer her question, but encouraged her to continue to pray for me and to ask God to lead me in the right direction. I didn't spend a lot of time on the phone with her because I sensed the conversation going in the direction of trying to make me feel guilty and ashamed enough to stay in the marriage. I respected her as a Godly woman, but did not need her to condemn me and accuse me of abandoning my family.

Asking for Special Prayer

During the most difficult times in our lives we should seek the prayers, guidance, and wisdom of Godly people. Many churches on Wednesday night and Sunday morning offer altar prayers for those who have special needs. During your time of difficulty, you should request special prayer from select prayer warriors, but don't necessarily take your needs before the entire congregation. I have seen people put their dirty laundry in the middle of the street by coming before the congregation saying, "I am asking for special prayer for me and my husband because you know we are going through a divorce." By doing something similar, you are opening yourself for trouble by inviting everyone's opinion in. You can't trust the opinion of everyone in the church.

Hopefully you have already talked with your pastor or his wife and asked them to pray for you. If you do speak with your pastor, be specific about what your current needs are. If you are part of a large church and do not have access to your spiritual leader, pray and ask God for His guidance and discernment to send someone you can talk to. Usually within a church family, there are godly people who can pray with you and for you. Keep the conversation simple, no one needs to know all of your business or every little detail in order to pray for you. All they need to know is you are in need of their prayers to help you through this difficult time.

Interference

During divorce two, because my husband was the pastor, I had no one inside the congregation I could ask for prayer directly. I sought another church to attend and quickly changed my membership. After attending the new church for a few months, my ex-husband attended a Christmas program our children were participating in. Our members greeted him with kindness and enjoyed having the opportunity to fellowship with him. My ex managed to leave quite an impression with those he interacted with. A woman in my congregation commented to me on how delightful my ex was. She indicated not being able to understand why we had gotten divorced, since we both seemed like such nice Christian people.

Now having met my ex-husband, she decided she was going to take it upon herself to pray us back together. Because she is such a faithful prayer warrior, she figured she could get the job done. Every time she saw me on Sundays and Wednesdays, she gladly commented with a smile, "I'm praying." After about the fifth or sixth time, I couldn't take it anymore and felt like I needed to say something. I finally got the courage to tell her, "It is very kind of you to pray for us, but please stop praying for us to get back together." Although I think I slightly offended her, she never mentioned praying for us again. However, she and her husband continued to encourage my children and often invited us over for holidays or Sunday dinner.

The greatest interference can come from your family, particularly your children. After all, children want their parents to be together, so you can be one big happy family. Keep in mind there are no ex-parents, only ex-spouses, and children are better served maintaining a relationship with both parents. Children struggle with the separation of their parents and find difficulty adjusting to new physical boundaries. Children may request the presence of the other parent for dinner or special occasions such as Christmas, Thanksgiving, or birthday celebrations.

On more than one occasion, my daughter added pictures of me and my ex as a couple on her art collages for show and tell. Even when she drew family pictures, she included both of us as though we were still married. To this day after being divorced for 15 years and remarried, she requests what she refers to as family shopping trips when we take her back to college every year.

My daughter used to watch a movie by the name of *Parent Trap,* where two identical twins manipulated their parents into getting back together. In another movie *House Arrest,* children lock their parents in the basement until they agree to work out their differences and stay married. I can't remember how many times we watched those movies. I also remember several conversations explaining to her that her dad and I were not getting back together.

Whether intervention, intercession, or interference, be aware of how you can be influenced by others. Don't open yourself up for just any kind of guidance. Know that anyone, if asked, has an opinion on your situation. Remember, requesting prayer from others is good, but be discerning in your conversations. In other words, pray before you ask others to pray for you. Pray that God will speak to you and that you will be able to recognize His voice. Whatever you do, don't mistake your own voice or the voices of others as God. If God is truly speaking to you, He will not lead you astray. Consider this scripture: "[God's voice may be heard] if there is for the hearer a messenger or an angel, an interpreter, one among a thousand, to show to man what is right for him [how to be upright and in right standing with God]" (Job 33:23, AMP).

Helpful Scriptures

As for you, don't pray for these people, don't cry out or plead for them, and don't intercede with me, for I won't listen to you. Jeremiah 7:16 (CEB)

This is why he can completely save those who are approaching God through him, because he always lives to speak with God for them. Hebrews 7:25 (CEB)

Devote yourselves to prayer, being watchful and thankful. Colossians 4:2 (NIV)

We always thank God for all of you when we mention you constantly in our prayers. This is because we remember your work that comes from faith, your effort that comes from love, and your perseverance that comes from hope in our Lord Jesus Christ in the presence of our God and Father. 1 Thessalonians 1:2-3 (CEB)

The apostles often met together and prayed with a single purpose in mind. The women and Mary the mother of Jesus would meet with them, and so would his brothers. Acts 1:14 (CEV)

"For where two or three are gathered in my name, I'm there with them." Matthew 18:20 (CEB)

CHAPTER 4
Christians Get Divorced?

Some Pharisees came to him to test him. They asked, "Is it lawful for a man to divorce his wife for any and every reason?" Matthew 19:3 (NIV)

Divorce Family History

At an early age, I learned that my brother was not my father's son. At first I didn't understand why he did not live with us in our childhood home in Tulsa, Oklahoma. Instead, my brother Tony lived with my maternal grandparents in the small town of Berlin, Maryland. When I became old enough to ask questions of adults, I soon learned that my mother had married another man right after high school and he was my brother's biological father. Most of my teenage years into adult life, I wanted to ask Mom about her first marriage experience, but I was too afraid. I was in my forties when I finally got the courage to ask Mom about her first marriage. She was more than happy to explain to me that she had gotten pregnant and married too early. Before she gave birth to my brother, she realized the marriage was a mistake, and the marriage was quickly dissolved following my brother's birth. My mother was still young and because her parents wanted the best for her, they encouraged her to go to college. My grandparents cared for my brother while Mom attended college. My mother met my father while in college and they were married for almost 60 years before Mom passed away.

Growing up, it was very important to my mother that we were nurtured in a religious environment, which meant we spent a lot of time at church. It was not uncommon for us to spend several hours a week at the church. During weekends and summer vacations, we attended regular youth meetings locally and throughout the states of Oklahoma and Arkansas. Mom attended a Methodist church and Dad was a hit and miss member of a Catholic church; however, we attended church with our mother. We were involved in activities such as the youth choir and youth usher board. Everyone knew and respected my mother and we were familiar with all of the families at church. Our church was a small community within itself and we had visited many of our member's homes for dinner or playtime. Many families may have been raising children that were not their own, but I wasn't aware of any one who was divorced. I didn't have any friends whose parents got divorced. Because everyone we were acquainted with was for the most part Christian families, I had concluded in my mind that Christians didn't get divorced. After all, from a very young age I consistently heard, "The family that prays together stays together."

My first real experience with divorce occurred while I was a college freshman in Maryland. The college I attended was not very far from where my grandparents lived, so I occasionally visited them for the weekend. During a visit I eavesdropped on a conversation between my grandmother and grandfather and learned my aunt and uncle (my mom's brother) who resided in New Jersey were getting a divorce. Once I returned to school I called Mom collect to find out what was going on. She confirmed that my aunt and uncle were getting a divorce. I was surprised for two reasons. Number one, my uncle was a minister, and two, I thought my aunt was one of the most beautiful women I knew. I acquainted their divorce with living the fast paced life in and around New York City. Preachers breaking up with their beautiful wives never happened in Oklahoma, only on television.

My uncle's children, a daughter and a son, were also in colleges nearby, and we often met up at our grandparent's home and hung out for the weekend. Late one Friday night or actually early Saturday morning, my cousins and I were out eating breakfast after partying at a club in Ocean City, Maryland. They didn't talk much about the divorce, but told me that their dad was planning to marry someone else. I was just getting used to the idea that my aunt and uncle were getting divorced and was not ready to hear about another marriage. Later I met my new Aunt Jane and I have come to love her just as much and have often visited with them in New Jersey and now in Maryland where they have retired.

Divorce in the Church

Single parenting was evident in the church I grew up in, but the word divorce was never mentioned. I was in my final years of college when I began to observe couples within the church going their separate ways. Couples I had babysat for as a teenager were getting divorced. I was extremely confused as I thought all of them were perfect families. Most of the couples attended our church regularly, so I assumed they were Christians.

In my mind, the young families I babysat for were living dream lives. They lived in large, brand new houses, had only one or two children, had great careers, and drove new cars. Because I babysat for them often on Friday and Saturday nights, I assumed they also had great social lives. They paid well for babysitting and I loved spending the night at their houses. I often relaxed in their fine homes wanting to be just like them when I grew up. It was devastating to me to learn they were divorcing. Sooner or later, one or both of them would leave the church and I would not be able to babysit for them when I returned home for summer break.

Divorce within the church is relatively common. In today's times, divorced church goers have fewer stigmas than in my parents' generation. Does going to church actually prevent couples from a marital breakup? Some researchers suggest Christianity protects couples from divorce, while others have found the same divorce rates among individuals professing to be Christians as those who indicate they are not Christians. The Barna Group has collected extensive data on Christians including divorce statistics. According to Barna, the divorce rate for Christians is 33 percent, with Catholics having the lowest rate.

Donald Hughes, author of e-book *The Divorce Reality*, supports the notion that Christians believe that Christianity protects them from getting a divorce. He attests that being born again does not protect married couples from having the same problems as the non-saved in marriages. According to Hughes, 90 percent of divorces among born-again couples occur after they became Christians.

Having been married to a pastor, I know for certain that being a Christian is not an automatic protector against getting a divorce. I also know from experience that couples who are struggling in their marriages are often afraid to admit their problems to their fellow church members. We pretended to be the perfect couple, all the while suffering in silence. Having a safe place where we could talk openly about our issues may have helped us to discover we were not alone.

Often as Christian leaders, we get caught up in trying to appear perfect and blessed. We are afraid to open up about our marital issues because of what others will think of us. Worse is the fear of being excommunicated from the church. I have heard of individuals being asked to leave the church or step down from their positions of leadership due to divorce. Prayerfully, this is not the case for you. Pastors and church leaders must accept the fact that divorce happens and minister to families where they are. Trained and equipped churches can provide a safe place for couples to seek help for their troubled marriages. Look around you, there may be several divorced individuals in your congregation. You are not the first Christian to consider divorce or need help in your marriage. The church is supposed to be a place where you can find love and forgiveness. Hopefully, your church will be a place of support and encouragement for you. "Are you tired? Worn out? Burned out on religion? Come to me. Get away with me and you'll recover your life. I'll show you how to take a real rest. Walk with me and work with me – watch how I do it. Learn the unforced rhythms of grace. I won't lay anything heavy or ill-fitting on you. Keep company with me and you'll learn to live freely and lightly" (Matthew 11:28-30, CEV).

Helpful Scriptures

Elders should be without fault. They should be faithful to their spouse, and have faithful children who can't be accused of self-indulgence or rebelliousness.
Titus 1:6 (CEB)

My friends, you surely understand enough about law to know that laws only have power over people who are alive. For example, the Law says that a man's wife must remain his wife as long as he lives. But once her husband is dead, she is free to marry someone else. However, if she goes off with another man while her husband is still alive, she is said to be unfaithful. Romans 7:1-3 (CEV)

The Pharisees asked Jesus, "Why did Moses say that a man could write out divorce papers and send his wife away?" Jesus replied, "You are so heartless! That's why Moses allowed you to divorce your wife. But from the beginning God did not intend it to be that way.
Matthew 19:7-8 (CEV)

The righteous live with integrity; happy are their children who come after them. Proverbs 20:7 (CEB)

Chapter 5
What the Bible Really Says About Divorce

What therefore God hath joined together, let not man put asunder. Matthew 19:6 (KJV)

Divorce is becoming a common word in today's society. According to the U.S. Census Bureau, about two and a half million people across all social and economic groups divorce each year. Individuals have either been divorced themselves, are children of divorced parents, or are the parents of divorced children. The formal definition of divorce is "the severing of the marital covenant by a legal decree and the sundering of the relationship; total separation; disunion." Divorce means different things to different people, but in the Christian setting many will indicate that divorce is not a good thing.

Being a church member for many years, some sermons and lessons regarding divorce have appeared harsh and condemning. While going through my divorce and after the process was over, I was fearful of the pastor preaching sermons that applied to my failed marriage. Somehow, a Sunday school lesson on divorce or rules concerning marriage came around at least twice a year. Whenever the dreaded lessons reappeared, I was uncomfortable in my Sunday school class thinking everyone was looking at me to see how I was going to respond.

As a Sunday school teacher, I was more uncomfortable. At the church where I attended following divorce two, the Sunday school teachers met midweek to go over the lesson before teaching on Sunday. One week while preparing, I noticed the dreaded lesson was coming up. I was terrified of attending the teacher's meeting because the lead Sunday school superintendent was known for being really hard on divorcees. Not going to the meeting was not an option, because you weren't supposed to teach if you had not attended the preparation meeting. I prayed our instructor would not embarrass and humiliate me because practically anything could send me out the door crying. My prayers were answered as I didn't feel singled out or embarrassed, thus I survived the class. However, I was still so nervous about teaching the lesson, I forgot to move my clock forward for daylight savings time and missed Sunday school altogether. I couldn't win for losing. When I arrived at church an hour late, I imagined everyone assumed I didn't come to Sunday school because I was divorced and not qualified to teach the lesson. Of course all of this was in my head and no one said anything. Thank God!

What's a Biblical Divorce?

I was once asked if my divorce was biblical. What on earth is a biblical divorce? When I asked around, the most typical answer was, "A biblical divorce means someone has committed adultery." If a spouse has committed adultery, the other person is released from the marriage if they choose to leave. God would not hold it against them. I have always been taught to read the Bible for myself and not to allow others to interpret the scriptures for me, so I did my own Biblical research.

Divorce is mentioned roughly 33 times in the Bible. In the Old Testament, divorce could be allowed for two reasons: sexual immorality and the man's decision. If a spouse was guilty of sexual immorality divorce was permitted. For instance, if a man married a women and found out that she was not a virgin when they married, he could divorce her by giving her a decree of divorce. The second type of divorce is described in Deuteronomy 24. A man could simply find his wife displeasing and give her a certificate of divorce. It was like divorce on demand. I had heard about the sexual immorality stuff, but had no idea a man could just decide he didn't want to be married anymore and send his wife away. There didn't seem to be many options for women in those days. A man could just decide he didn't want to be married to a woman anymore. Perhaps he didn't like what she was wearing one day and decided to divorce her? Or maybe she burned his dinner or gained weight after having his children? Either way, all he had to do was to give her a certificate of divorce and send her on her way.

A book entitled *Divorce and Remarriage in the Church* by David Instone-Brewer was written for pastors and church leaders to help them counsel on the many questions Christians have about divorce and remarriage. You may want to recommend the book to your pastor or marriage ministry leader. The book reviewed the damage of the no-fault divorce amongst Christians, leading them to divorce for any reason. Instone-Brewer also speaks about Jesus' views on divorce. He even reminds us that Jesus understands because his parents almost never married.

As you can see, divorce is a hot topic not only in the Bible but in the church as well. Today is no different in that many Christian's have different views on divorce. My advice is to study the scriptures yourself and seek God for answers. I agree with Jesus, you should not divorce just because you don't want to be married anymore. In fact I don't believe you should run straight to the courthouse because your spouse has been unfaithful. I have seen numerous couples survive infidelity and come through stronger than ever. I have also seen some forgive their spouse over and over for the same sexual sins. Stop and take inventory of why you are divorcing. What is your two minute speech as to why you are going your separate ways?

I have seen abuse happen in marriages and cannot with a clean conscience encourage anyone to stay in an abusive marriage. If abuse is going on in your marriage, seek help immediately from a qualified professional. Help may include law enforcement and/or counseling from a counselor or a pastor. Whatever you do, please do not suffer in silence. God will never leave you or forsake you, so trust His guidance to lead you to someone who can help you.

A Christian man or woman may marry someone who is unsaved hoping they will change him or her. Years have passed and nothing has changed for the spouse spiritually. The question was asked of Jesus if couples should stay together if they are unequally yoked, meaning one is a Christian and one is not. The Bible addresses it this way in 1 Corinthians 7:13-14, "As long as the nonbelieving spouse is willing to stay, the believer should stay in the marriage, because the presence of the believer blesses and gives hope to the nonbeliever and also blesses the children in the marriage." If your spouse is not saved, don't give up hope. I have seen miracles happen and finally the unsaved one comes to Christ. Some couples married while unequally yoked and later divorced. When the unsaved partner came to Christ the couples remarried and had much stronger marriages.

If people ask you if your divorce is biblical, find a nice way to tell them it is none of their business. However, you may want to have a different conversation with your pastor and ask him to pray with you and for you. Find a prayer partner who can give you Godly advice and pray with you through the process. Select someone who will be honest with you and not just tell you what you want to hear. If your confidante replies with, "If I were you I would leave," they may not necessarily be an objective resource for you. He or she should be asking you the hard questions, not just agreeing with everything you say. Most of all he or she should not be creating more problems for you. "Yes, each of us will give a personal account to God. So let's stop condemning each other. Decide instead to live in such a way that you will not cause another believer to stumble and fall" (Romans 14:12-13, NLT).

Helpful Scriptures

And if a woman has a husband who is not a believer and he is willing to live with her, she must not divorce him. For the unbelieving husband has been sanctified through his wife, and the unbelieving wife has been sanctified through her believing husband. Otherwise your children would be unclean, but as it is, they are holy.
1 Corinthians 7:13-14 (NIV)

If a man marries a woman who becomes displeasing to him because he finds something indecent about her, and he writes her a certificate of divorce, gives it to her and sends her from his house, and if after she leaves his house she becomes the wife of another man, and her second husband dislikes her and writes her a certificate of divorce, gives it to her and sends her from his house, or if he dies, then her first husband, who divorced her, is not allowed to marry her again after she has been defiled. That would be detestable in the eyes of the LORD. Do not bring sin upon the land the LORD your God is giving you as an inheritance.
Deuteronomy 24: 1-4 (NIV)

I say that if your wife has not committed some terrible sexual sin, you must not divorce her to marry someone else. If you do, you are unfaithful." The disciples said, "If that's how it is between a man and a woman, it's better not to get married." Matthew 19:7-10 (CEV)

CHAPTER 6
Is Divorce a Sin?

Jesus said to the woman, "your faith has saved you. Go in peace." Luke 7:50 (CEB)

Divorce is a Sin

Based on what I have read in the Bible, divorce is a sin. Because I am divorced twice, I have sinned twice. I get it. I don't need others to remind me. I didn't need anyone else to make me feel guilty; I did a good job of self-condemnation. The guilt and shame consumed me at times. Every time I heard the word divorce, I felt a sense of shame that I had committed one of the worst sins possible. Even though I could rationalize the divorce wasn't totally my fault, I felt God was not happy with my choices. The guilt was even worse the second time around. Would I ever be worthy in God's eyes again? Could I be forgiven for getting a divorce?

The public humiliation was challenging whether it was real or imagined. I felt like Hester Prynne in the movie *The Scarlet Letter* who was forced to wear the letter A on her dress as a symbol of her shame. Instead I wore an invisible D on my forehead and was consumed with what others thought of me. Having been married to a really great pastor and no longer wanting to be married to him, of course, left others with the conclusion that I was the guilty party. "Surely, it must be her," I imagined the crowds saying. A female at my former church made the following comments to a friend. "Women like her mess it up for the rest of us. She had a nice guy and she didn't want him. What else could she want?"

Again, I made a lot of assumptions and created my own guilt and shame. I assumed my neighbors were talking about us, not seeing my husband coming and going from the house. I believed everyone at church looked at me differently. All of the guilt began to affect my spiritual life. As I read the Bible I struggled with whether or not God could or would forgive me. No one took the time to share with me that God still loves you after you get a divorce. It was even difficult to pray as I felt judged by God because of the failure to keep the marriage vows of "till death do us part."

Some argue that if the divorce is biblical, it is not a sin. Is that the reason why people asked me if my divorce was biblical? Whatever. If someone asks you this question, please kindly tell them to pray and ask God themselves, then walk away.

A Sin is a Sin

We all have heard the statements "a sin is a sin" and "all sin is the same in God's eyes." I don't want to start a philosophical argument, but think about the other sins you have committed in your lifetime. Perhaps you have told some lies. Perhaps you cheated on your taxes or failed to tithe. Perhaps you gossip regularly. What if we haven't followed all of the Ten Commandments? The definition of sin as I have been taught is "missing the mark" or doing anything against God's will. Sin is also viewed as anything that violates the ideal relationship between a person and

God; or as any diversion from the ideal order for human living. I have heard the following: Worrying is a sin. Gambling is a sin. Adultery is a sin. Abortion is a sin. Suicide is a sin. Gossip is a sin. Pride is a sin. Gluttony is a sin. The list goes on and on as to what is and isn't a sin. Crimes against others including theft and murder are regarded as sins and may be considered greater than others. All sin deserves God's judgment, but not all receive the same judgment. We can easily create problems for ourselves in attempting to justify our sins. Any sin can lead you to hell without the grace and forgiveness given to us only through the blood of Jesus.

God Hates the Sin but Loves the Sinner

The story of King David gives a clear example of God hating sin but loving the sinner. David was guilty of some of the most serious sins recorded in the Old Testament. His transgressions included lust, adultery, lying, murder, and pride. The acknowledgement of his sins caused him to be repentant. Psalm 51 is David's confession and his cry for mercy and forgiveness.

> *Have mercy upon me, O God, according to your loving kindness; According to the multitude of your tender mercies, blot out my transgressions. Wash me thoroughly from my iniquity, and cleanse me from my sin. For I acknowledge my transgressions, and my sin is always before me. Against You, You only, have I sinned, and done this evil in Your sight—That You may be found just when You speak and blameless when You judge.* Psalms 51:1-4 (ASV)

It took much time, study, and prayer for me to realize divorce is a sin just like any other area of my life where I have gone against God's will. But guess what? God can and does forgive. The good news is every sin—no matter how large or small—can be forgiven and engulfed by God's unlimited sea of grace. God offers salvation to those who have sinned. We have clear instructions on what to do when we have sinned. I John 1:9 reminds us that if we ask for forgiveness, God is faithful and just to forgive us and then cleanse us from all unrighteousness. It has been said that God hates sin, but loves the sinner. This has never been truer than when a Christian experiences divorce. God not only forgives us but he draws us closer to Him in our trouble and restores the sweet fellowship broken by our rebellion.

Therefore, let us come boldly to the throne of grace where God has promised to help us in our time of need (Hebrews 4:10). This is not the first sin we have committed and it won't be the last. Divorce is a season in which we need the mercy and grace of God. The throne of grace represents authority, esteem, and reverence. Even the worst of sinners can approach the throne with the encouragement that we will be met by a loving and forgiving God. Asking in faith, God will put his arms around us, as we would our repentant children wanting to restore fellowship with us when they have done wrong. God is willing to forgive all!

I am forever grateful for God's loving kindness, mercy, and grace extended to me. I am thankful to have been released from the burden of guilt whether self-inflicted or placed upon me by others. Guilt can become an unforgiving taskmaster that drives us away from God. Or as in David's case, our guilt can lead us to restore a right relationship with Him. How we respond to guilt can determine our success in life for years to come. Always remember that we are covered by the blood of Jesus: Therefore, there is now no condemnation for those who are in Christ Jesus, because through Christ Jesus the law of the Spirit who gives life has set you free from the law of sin and death (Romans 8:1-2, NIV).

Helpful Scriptures

If a man divorces his wife, and after she leaves him marries another, can he return to her again? Wouldn't such an act completely corrupt the land? Yet you have prostituted yourself with many lovers. Would you return to me? declares the LORD. Jeremiah 3:1 (CEB)

I'm passing on the Lord's command to those who are married: A wife shouldn't leave her husband, but if she does leave him, then she should stay single or be reconciled to her husband. And a man shouldn't divorce his wife. 1 Corinthians 7:10-11 (CEB)

The one whose wrongdoing is forgiven, whose sin is covered over, is truly happy! Psalm 32:1 (CEB)

You are kind, God! Please have pity on me. You are always merciful! Please wipe away my sins. Psalm 51:1 (CEV)

God rescued us from the dark power of Satan and brought us into the kingdom of his dear Son, who forgives our sins and sets us free. Colossians 1:13-14 (CEV)

Anyone who tries to keep all of the Law but fails at one point is guilty of failing to keep all of it. The one who said, Don't commit adultery, also said, Don't commit murder. So if you don't commit adultery but do commit murder, you are a lawbreaker. James 2:10-11 (CEB)

CHAPTER 7
It May Not Be About You

Be clearheaded. Keep alert. Your accuser, the devil, is on the prowl like a roaring lion, seeking someone to devour.
1 Peter 5:8 (CEB)

You may be so consumed with what is going on in your life that you may fail to realize that there is a spiritual war going on around you. If you are reading this book you are most likely a Christian. As a ministry couple, my ex-husband and I tried to be an example for others to look up to. If our marriage was destroyed, it could have a ripple effect on not only our immediate family, but also our church and our community. Many thought we were the perfect couple and became afraid for their own marriages. I can imagine them thinking, "If divorce can happen to them, we don't stand a chance."

In divorce one, my husband was an associate minister of the church he grew up in. After we were reconciled, he became the assistant pastor of the same church which had grown significantly. When divorce two occurred, we had relocated to Kansas City and he was the senior pastor of a growing church. My concern for his ministry led me to keep my mouth shut in hopes that the church could recover. I left the church quietly and did not think about the aftermath. I was more concerned about our children and their wellbeing.

After joining another church, I found out that the pastor and his wife had also went through a divorce. I was angry at God for allowing me to join a church where I would be reminded of my own failed marriage. I now believe God wanted me to see the devastating effect divorce amongst church leadership can have on a church family. As a result of my pastor's divorce, many members left the church, a few couples separated and later divorced, and the church attempted to remove the pastor as their leader. I had an opportunity to see firsthand how other people's lives were changed and how Satan used a leader's failed marriage to cause turmoil and upheaval within the church. Leaders rebelled, openly criticized and condemned the pastor, and made it their goal to destroy him.

Satan can use failed marriages not only to destroy other families, but also churches and communities. If you destroy the head, attacking the body is easy. Satan wants to do everything he can to ruin Christian testimonies and tear down families. When the family unit is damaged there is widespread loss emotionally, financially, and socially. Many of society's ills are a result of the breakdown of the family including teenage pregnancy, child abuse, poor school performance, depression, and poverty. Satan is determined to win the spiritual battle against God, and will use whoever he wants to help him.

Stop thinking about your own plight for a moment and think about whom else besides you and your spouse is affected by the dissolution of your marriage. What will be the outcome for your children? The Bible says that Satan desires to sift us like wheat (Luke 22:31). Maybe he wants to destroy your family name and destroy the generations that are to come after you. There may be a divine assignment on your life or a family member's and the devil does not want you to be successful. Maybe he wants to destroy your testimony and the fruits of your labor. What better way to destroy your standing in the church and the community?

Know that when you are on fire for the Lord, Satan will use every weapon he has to destroy you and your family. Satan knows that once the family unit is broken, the society and nation will struggle with unity. Accept the challenge and trust God that He will give you what you need to win the battle. Ask for discernment to see who your real enemy is. Most likely it is not your spouse. Even though I could not see the truth when I was going through, it is now clear that our problems were part of a larger battle between good and evil. Learn from my experiences and spend time in prayer, bible study, and meditation. Equip yourself with the whole armor of God so that you resist the devil and stand (Ephesians 6:11).

If your eyes have been opened as a result of reading this chapter, it is not too late to repair the damage in your marriage. My goal is to help you make the right decision. Remember, I wouldn't wish divorce on my worst enemy as it is equivalent to death. Stop and spend some quiet time with God asking Him to direct your thoughts and behaviors. Ask for discernment to see who the real enemy is. Accept the fact that this battle may not be against flesh and blood, particularly that of your spouse, but against the rulers of darkness. Stand your ground, submit yourself to God. Resist the devil, and he will run away from you (James 4:7).

Helpful Scriptures

'Simon, Simon, look! Satan has asserted the right to sift you all like wheat." Luke 22:31 (CEB)

The thief does not come except to steal, and to kill, and to destroy. I have come that they may have life, and that they may have it more abundantly. John 10:10 (NKJV)

Finally, be strengthened by the Lord and his powerful strength. Put on God's armor so that you can make a stand against the tricks of the devil. We aren't fighting against human enemies but against rulers, authorities, forces of cosmic darkness, and spiritual powers of evil in the heavens. Therefore, pick up the full armor of God so that you can stand your ground on the evil day and after you have done everything possible to still stand.
Ephesians 6:10-13 (CEB)

Don't worry about anything, but pray about everything. With thankful hearts offer up your prayers and requests to God. Then, because you belong to Christ Jesus, God will bless you with peace that no one can completely understand. And this peace will control the way you think and feel. Finally, my friends, keep your minds on whatever is true, pure, right, holy, friendly, and proper. Don't ever stop thinking about what is truly worthwhile and worthy of praise. Philippians 4:6-8 (CEV)

Chapter 8
Whose Fault Is It?

Both of them were righteous in the sight of God, observing all the Lord's commands and decrees blamelessly.
Luke 1:6 (NIV)

The number one question I received when informing others of my impending divorce was: "Whose fault is it?" Why did someone have the nerve to ask me this question? Why do people find the need to place the blame for divorce solely on one of the parties? There are only three ways to answer the question of fault: 1) It's my fault, 2) It's my partner's fault, or 3) We both take equal responsibility for our divorce.

If you are still angry with your spouse, you may be tempted to respond with answer number two, "It's my partner's fault." When you are furious with your spouse, blaming everything on them feels like the right thing to do. Perhaps your spouse filed for the divorce. Does the decision to file indicate whose fault it is? Perhaps it is not your fault and your spouse has requested the divorce and is determined to go through the process without your consent. Even worse, perhaps he or she has committed a sin that makes it legal or what we refer to as a biblical divorce. If a spouse is guilty of adultery, we are quick to quote Matthew 5:32 (NIV) which states, "Any man who divorces his wife except for sexual immorality causes his wife to commit adultery."

If you indicate the divorce was your fault, questions will follow as to what you did to destroy the marriage. As a result, you are blamed for not giving the marriage a chance and will find yourself constantly on the defensive. Once you are tired of attempting to preserve your reputation, eventually you may begin to place blame on the other person. It's funny how the tables turn when we find ourselves on the defensive.

Whenever I was asked the question of whose fault it was, I sometimes followed the question with a question: "Why does it have to be somebody's fault? It was a mutual decision between the two of us." Truth is, the first time my ex filed and the second time I filed. I guess we are even. Actually, I had more difficulty explaining why we remarried than why we were separating for the second time.

Fault and No Fault

A fault divorce requires one spouse to plead that the other has committed adultery, abandonment, felony, cruelty, or other similarly guilty acts. In the days before the no-fault divorce, a spouse had to prove that the other party had committed such acts in order for the judge to grant a divorce.

A no-fault divorce is the dissolution of a marriage that does not require a showing of wrongdoing by either party. When a couple determines that they can no longer get along and as a result want to divorce they can file "no-fault" based on incompatibility, also known as irreconcilable differences or irremediable breakdown of the marriage. The selection of no-fault allows the court to grant a divorce in response to a petition by either party without requiring the petitioner to provide evidence that the defendant has committed a breach of the marital contract.

Ronald Reagan, while the Governor of California, was the first to sign the California Family Law Act of 1969 which allowed a couple to file a no-fault divorce. Of course he may have had personal reasons as Reagan was divorced and remarried. Once the law was approved, couples in California were free to divorce on the grounds of irreconcilable differences. Fault was no longer required in order to obtain a divorce. Not long after California approved the no-fault divorce, other states followed suit. Since 1985, the no-fault divorce has been made available in all states across the nation. There are a few states which only allow no-fault divorces and will not allow a fault divorce, including Colorado, Washington D.C., Hawaii, Iowa, Kentucky, Michigan, Minnesota, Missouri, Montana, Washington, and Wisconsin.

Other than the states mentioned previously, most states still offer both fault and no-fault divorces. Again, if filing a fault divorce, proof must be present that the respondent has committed such acts as adultery, abusive treatment, excessive use of drugs or alcohol, imprisonment, abandonment, or straight up craziness! You won't believe what is allowed in Alabama and Utah. A spouse can file for divorce on the basis of impotence, if it is proven.

The length of time of separation also varies for states. For instance, if you live in Maryland or New York, either one spouse has to be at fault or the couple has to be separated for at least a year or more before the divorce can be granted. A very close friend of mine residing in Maryland had to wait over a year to divorce her drug abusing husband. Make sure you understand the laws of your resident state.

The use of the no-fault divorce has positive benefits for women. A study done by Stevenson and Wolfers at the Stanford Business School compared states with a higher rate of no-fault divorce and found a 20 percent reduction in female suicide and a 33 percent reduction in domestic violence against women. Thank God.

So what should you say when someone asks you whose fault it is? The correct answer is, "It's both of our faults, and we both played a role in the dissolution of our marriage." Save yourself some trouble and keep other people out of your business. You really don't owe any one an explanation, but if you have to say anything, mention incompatibility. Using irreconcilable differences indicates the fault lies with both of you equally.

If you decided to go the fault route because of horrible behaviors by your spouse, be prepared to prove your claims. Be careful in your attempt to prove that your spouse is the scum of the earth. In proving he or she is such a horrible person, you could end up causing irrevocable damage to your children. Remember your children have blood from both of you, and your children may exhibit character traits similar to your spouse. By badmouthing your spouse in public you can accidentally ruin your children's self-esteem. Besides, you may end up spending a lot of money and energy focusing on the negative. However, if you think it's worth it, get yourself a good lawyer and hang on for a tumultuous ride.

Helpful Scriptures

'Why do you look at the speck of sawdust in your brother's eye and pay no attention to the plank in your own eye? How can you say to your brother, 'Let me take the speck out of your eye,' when all the time there is a plank in your own eye? You hypocrite, first take the plank out of your own eye, and then you will see clearly to remove the speck from your brother's eye." Matthew 7:3-5 (NIV)

Look at how they lie in ambush for my life! Powerful people are attacking me, LORD—but not because of any error or sin of mine. They run and take their stand— but not because of any fault of mine. Get up when I cry out to you! Look at what's happening! Psalms 59:3-4 (CEB)

Blessed are those whose ways are blameless, who walk according to the law of the LORD. Psalm 119:1 (NIV)

He reserves ability for those with integrity. He is a shield for those who live a blameless life. Proverbs 2:7 (CEB)

Now unto him that is able to keep you from falling, and to present you faultless before the presence of his glory with exceeding joy. Jude 1:24 (KJV)

I pray this so that you will be able to decide what really matters and so you will be sincere and blameless on the day of Christ. Philippians 1:10 (CEB)

CHAPTER 9
Failed at Marriage More Than Once?

The woman replied, "I don't have a husband." "You are right to say, 'I don't have a husband,'" Jesus answered. "You've had five husbands, and the man you are with now isn't your husband. You've spoken the truth."
John 4:17-18 (CEB)

I could not believe I was standing in front of a judge for the second time, going through divorce all over again. What didn't I learn the first time around? Lord, are you trying to tell me that I am just not cut out to be married? Perhaps I should have paid attention to Paul's advice in 1 Corinthians 7:38, indicating that it is perfectly alright to marry, but it is better not to get married at all. Divorce court was the last place I wanted to be. Nonetheless, I was thankful we were living in a different state this time around. Imagine having the same judge twice.

It's not extremely difficult to explain why you got a divorce the first time. According to Jennifer Baker of the Forest Institute of Professional Psychology in Springfield, Missouri, 50 percent of all first marriages will end in divorce. Typical explanations include: we were young when we married; he cheated on me; I just seem to attract losers; or we just grew apart. If all else fails, just blame it on the ex.

Explaining to others how my ex-husband and I got back together the first time didn't require a lot of explanation. We just talked about the mistakes we both made the first time around and the lessons we learned. I remember having conversations with others when we remarried and talking about all of the areas we had corrected. In fact, our church did an article on us, praising God for the miracle of bringing us back together. Now that we were back into the divorce process; I felt I was ruined! How was I going to get over the embarrassment of admitting we made a mistake in remarrying and were divorcing for the second time?

I thought I had figured out what went wrong in our first marriage and never thought divorce would happen to us again. Now my chances seemed bleak for ever marrying again. Who would ever consider marrying a woman who had been married and divorced twice? Several marriages may work for rich women and movie stars like Zsa Zsa Gabor who has married nine times, but not for a divorced preacher's wife. Of course, no one blamed the preacher, they blamed his Jezebel wife!

Have you been married and divorced more than once? Are you like myself and failed at marriage once again? Maybe you are on your third divorce. I recently spoke with a dear friend who indicated that he was now going through his third divorce. I have numerous friends who have failed at marriage more than once. According to Jennifer Baker of the Forest Institute of Professional Psychology in Springfield, Missouri, 67 percent of all second marriages will end in divorce, and 74 percent of all third marriages will end in divorce. The more times you marry the greater the risk for divorce.

If you are like me, you thought when you married the second time that you had learned some valuable lessons from your first marriage and weren't planning to repeat the same mistakes. In my case, I thought we had worked out all of the bugs while we were apart. I had even gone to a divorce support group to work through my own issues before marrying again. I wondered why God would let divorce happen to me not once, but twice.

I'm Through with Marriage

Has being divorced more than once or twice caused you to want to give up on marriage? Do you find yourself saying, "Perhaps, I am not marriage material"? Do you feel like you are making poor choices when it comes to selecting a mate? To save face, it is easy to just decide you are done with marriage and proclaim you will never, ever, try it again. The wall goes up, and if anyone mentions the word again, you will shut them down. A close friend experienced a very painful divorce and never wanted to marry again. After being single for two years, she met a wonderful man whom she grew to love very dearly. She admitted her love for him, but was afraid that marriage would ruin their relationship, so she made the choice to live with him instead. Every time he brought up marriage, she avoided the questions all together or simply told him no.

Even after divorcing two times, I still believe in marriage. Though I wasn't looking for a husband, my prayer was that one day the Lord would bless me with the man He created just for me. My hope for you is that you do not give up on love or give up on yourself just because you have failed once, twice, or even three times. I remarried four years later and this time really know that God ordained our marriage. I am thankful for not only a second chance, but a third chance.

Celebrities do it all the time, and no one seems to care. Did you know that Larry King had been married eight times and Geraldo Rivera has been married five times? When we think of multiple marriages in Hollywood, Elizabeth Taylor comes to mind. She married a total of eight times to seven different men. Wondering why the math doesn't seem to add up? Guess what? Liz married and divorced Richard Burton and then they tied the knot again. Not surprisingly, their second union didn't stick either. Elizabeth Taylor's life has become the all-time marriage joke. Ministers open their sermons with the phrase, "Like Elizabeth Taylor said to her 7th husband, I won't keep you long."

Have you learned from your failed marriages and relationships? Should you be concerned with the count? Actress and singer Chanté Moore released a book entitled *Will I Marry Me?* In her book she discusses having failed at marriage three times and the lessons learned. Even though I married the same man twice, when my children or anyone else decide to search my public records, they will find three marriages and two divorces. While married to my first husband the second time, a church member was featuring an article on us and wanted to know our anniversary date. I gave her both dates. She questioned if I should include both dates because of what the members might think. I assured her that we were proud of the fact that we were able to reconcile after having gone all the way to divorce court. We wanted our experience to encourage and help others.

There is an oldie but goody song that indicates the second time around is better than the first time. This statement held true for me on my second trip to divorce court. I already knew what to expect and I was determined not to cry. Because it was Valentine's Day, I wasn't worried about running into anyone I knew. I just wanted everything to be over with so I could move on with my life. My hope was that a better life would await me.

Meet the Woman at the Well

Read the story of the woman at the well found in John 4:3-30. She has no name because she could be any of us. Jesus went out of his way to stop by and minister to her. Her reputation caused her to come to the well during the middle of the day because she didn't want to be seen or bothered by others. Perhaps they were talking about her because she had been married and divorced several times. Perhaps she had no friends who were willing to be seen with her.

Meeting Jesus, he acknowledged to her that she had been married five times and was currently living in adultery. But guess what? Other than mentioning where she was, He did not condemn her, however He offered to redeem her by offering living water. This is the only place in the Bible where Jesus ministers to one who is divorced. Notice Jesus doesn't condemn her for her failed marital history, instead he exhibits compassion and grace. As a result of this woman meeting Jesus, an entire city is saved.

From that city many of the Samaritans believed in Him because of the word of the woman who testified, "He told me all the things that I have done." So when the Samaritans came to Jesus, they were asking Him to stay with them; and He stayed there two more days. Many more believed because of His word; and they were saying to the woman, "It is no longer because of what you said that we believe, for we have heard for ourselves and know that this One is indeed the Savior of the world." (John 4:39-42 (ASV)

I agree with author Richard Crooks in his book *Finding God in the Seasons of Divorce.* This woman managed to lead more people to Christ on her one testimony than many others. God managed to use a divorced woman, not one who was only divorced one time, but someone who had been married five times. She is the one that made a difference for so many people.

After much prayer and insight, God has turned my mess into a message and my failure into faith. Having experienced divorce twice, I can be a support to someone going through their own struggles. If you have been married and divorced more than once, take heart, Jesus still loves you and always will.

Helpful Scriptures

My days have passed, my plans are shattered. Yet the desires of my heart turn night into day; in the face of the darkness light is near. Job 17:11-12 (NIV)

A person's steps are made secure by the LORD when they delight in his way. Though they trip up, they won't be thrown down, because the LORD holds their hand. Psalms 37:23-24 (CEB)

Don't be a cruel person who attacks good people and hurts their families. Even if good people fall seven times, they will get back up. But when trouble strikes the wicked, that's the end of them. Don't be happy to see your enemies' trip and fall down. Proverbs 24:15-17 (CEV)

Jesus told her, "Go and bring your husband." The woman answered, "I don't have a husband." "That's right," Jesus replied, "you're telling the truth. You don't have a husband. You have already been married five times, and the man you are now living with isn't your husband." The woman said, "Sir, I can see that you are a prophet. John 4:16-19 (CEV)

Even if good people fall seven times, they will get back up. But when trouble strikes the wicked, that's the end of them. Proverbs 24:16 (CEV)

CHAPTER 10
Separation

You go one way, and I'll go the other." Then they left in separate directions. 1 Kings 18:6 (CEV)

Often the first activity to happen when a couple is considering divorce is separation. Separation from your spouse does not always mean living at separate addresses. There are couples who have been estranged for years living in the same house. In divorce one, my husband and I were in a hurry to be away from one another physically. Within a few days of our decision to be apart, he moved in with his brother until he got an apartment. He didn't incur any immediate expenses by going out right away and getting an apartment. In divorce two, once we made the decision to divorce, we agreed to sell the house first and then find separate residences.

While waiting for the house to sell, we agreed that I would remain in the master bedroom and he would move downstairs to the basement area. This arrangement was workable because his office was in the basement and there was a full bathroom as well. Fortunately, we found a buyer within four weeks of putting our house on the market. Even though we were still in the same house, we began to live separate lives; however, we worked together to manage our children's schedules. I continued to cook family meals and left a plate for him whenever he arrived home. When we finally moved out, he and his friends assisted me in moving to my new residence.

The definition of separation in relation to divorce is to stop living together without getting a divorce. According to divorce attorney expert Emily Doskow, there are three kinds of separation:

TRIAL SEPARATION: living apart while deciding whether to divorce.
PERMANENT SEPARATION: living apart with the intention to divorce.
LEGAL SEPARATION: includes orders about property division, alimony, child custody, and support.

Sometimes, due to financial constraints or complexities related to children, a couple cannot move to different addresses right away. Occasionally couples are involved in property battles and both parties refuse to move out. Again, some states require a designated length of time of separation before a couple can file for divorce.

There may be several reasons why couples separate. Susan Pease Gadoua, in an article written for *Psychology Today*, indicates three reasons: as a step in the divorce process; to gain perspective on the marriage; or to enhance the marriage.

Some couples are able to live apart for a small amount of time and find being apart is therapeutic and ultimately the marriage is strengthened. As the saying goes, absence makes the heart grow fonder.

If the purpose of the separation is to enhance the marriage, it is important that the time be spent wisely. Do the work required to heal your marriage. Engage the assistance of a qualified marriage counselor to help you work through the process. Set reasonable expectations, lay out some ground rules, and maintain regular contact with your spouse. For example, make an agreement to separate for three months, but plan to meet once a week to work through issues, one at a time. The average length of separation should be no longer than six months. Staying apart longer than six months may be a sign that the marriage will end. The time away from one another works for some couples and the marriage becomes stronger. I have seen this practice work for quite a few couples.

Those who are attempting to gain a better perspective on their marriage must commit to doing the work. Spend some time talking about expectations, realities, and determine goals for the marriage. A separation can be an expensive endeavor, so it is best to gain the perspective while living under the same roof. Some decide to work out their differences, once they experience the difficulties and expenses of establishing separate residences and shuffling children back and forth.

It is best not to separate if you are just using the process to make the divorce process gentler or using the time apart as an excuse to do what you want to do. Separation will not work if there is a huge amount of distrust between the two spouses. I have watched some couples use the separation process to pursue other relationships. Getting involved in another relationship is a huge mistake. Doing so means you are most likely not trying to repair your marriage. If you have given up on the marriage admit it and don't deceive your spouse.

Separation Agreement

If you are using separation as the first step toward divorce it is probably best to file for a legal separation. A lawyer can officially prepare what is called a Separation Agreement which is a legally binding contract between the two spouses at the time of separation. The document outlines issues such as child custody/access, property, debts, and child support. It is always best to have the agreement designed by an attorney.

Once the separation agreement is in place you can begin the process of filing for divorce. Some couples are happy being apart and never file the divorce decree. I have met individuals who have been legally separated for 20 years and have not taken the necessary steps to complete the divorce process. They almost forget they have never filed for divorce until a legal issue arises or one decides they want to marry someone else.

Who Should Move?

If you are unsure of the expected length of time of your separation, it may be best for the primary caregiver, whether male or female, to remain in the home with the children while the other spouse relocates temporarily. Shop around for a short term lease. Moving is a pain, so relocating one person is easier than moving everyone. Besides, if the marriage improves and you reconcile, your home has not been completely disrupted. Remaining in the same location may help ease children's fears of losing everything. This arrangement will only work if the spouse who has moved can continue to contribute financially to the household.

Be strategic with the separation time. Spend time in prayer and reflection to determine if you are making the right decision. Remember separation does not have to be final. However, if divorce is the next step, begin preparing yourself for the next stages. Put your seatbelt on, and get ready for a bumpy ride.

Helpful Scriptures

But I will rescue them and no longer let them be mistreated. I will separate the good from the bad. Ezekiel 34:22 CEV)

This was the first time the LORD had told Moses to command the people of Israel to move on. Numbers 10:13 (CEV)

Then they are no longer two people, but one. And no one should separate a couple that God has joined together." Matthew 19:6 (CEV)

I am sure that nothing can separate us from God's love— not life or death, not angels or spirits, not the present or the future, and not powers above or powers below. Nothing in all creation can separate us from God's love for us in Christ Jesus our Lord! Romans 8:38-39 (CEV)

Abram said to Lot, "We are close relatives. We shouldn't argue, and our men shouldn't be fighting one another. There is plenty of land for you to choose from. Let's separate. If you go north, I'll go south; if you go south, I'll go north." Genesis 13:8-9 (CEV)

She will run after her lovers, but not catch them; she will search, but not find them. Then she will say, "I'll return to my first husband. Life was better then." Hosea 2:7

DURING DIVORCE
The Good, the Bad, and the Ugly

Chapter 11
Timing

Everything on earth has its own time and its own season. There is a time for birth and death, planting and reaping, for killing and healing, destroying and building, for crying and laughing, weeping and dancing, for throwing stones and gathering stones, embracing and parting. There is a time for finding and losing, keeping and giving, for tearing and sewing, listening and speaking. There is also a time for love and hate, for war and peace.
Ecclesiastes 3:1-8 (CEV)

Is There a Good Time to Divorce?

Why now? Why am I going through this now? Why couldn't this wait until next year, or why didn't it happen last year? We just bought a new house. This is bad timing. Truth is, there is never a perfect time for a divorce. No day of the week, month of the year, or season in one's life is optimal for this life altering event. The dissolution of a marriage can come when life seems to be going perfectly well, when you are sitting on the mountaintop, or it can rear its ugly head when you are already down in the valley feeling like you can't take any more misfortune.

My first divorce came right before Christmas. What a way to ruin a child's holidays. My second divorce occurred following a vacation to Cancun, Mexico, where we had purchased a very expensive wedding ring. There is no way we would have made such a huge purchase if we had forecasted divorce in our future. The court date was scheduled for Valentine's Day. Nothing says love on Valentine's Day like a final divorce decree being granted.

Different professionals offer a variety of opinions. In relation to children, lawyers have suggested for couples to wait until children are in high school because one will be required to pay child support until the children complete their education. Others claim the emotional turmoil experienced by children can be reduced by waiting to divorce after children are adults and out of the home. Financial experts suggest waiting until your credit scores are higher or when debt is lowest.

Believe it or not, I read an article posted on the Huffington Post that indicated more people make decisions about divorce at the beginning of the year. Divorce lawyers have observed this pattern and are now using this knowledge to their advantage and advertise accordingly. Some of the reasons for the increase during the first of the year are because individuals may make New Year's resolutions to get a divorce. Some realize during the holidays that they refuse to end another year the same way and thus begin the divorce process. For others, the timing wasn't right during the holidays perhaps because they were being protective of their children. Therefore, they will wait until the holidays are over and file as soon as possible.

Some couples stay together until the end of the year because of the tax benefits. They can file taxes as married and get the deductions. With all of the financial information that has to be gathered, it is somewhat easier to gather the documents at the same time one is gathering information for taxes. All this documentation is usually available by the end of January when W-2's are received.

Divorce Process Timeline

How long is the divorce process? The length depends on the nature of the divorce and how civil the couple is. Having children, a lot of property, and other challenges can stretch the process out. In the case of a no-fault divorce, the process could move as quickly as six months. Fault divorces where one spouse is accused of adultery, cruelty, desertion, or something else that may be contested, may take six months to a year to reach litigation.

To save time, many couples file a no-fault divorce based on incompatibility. A legal separation is often the beginning. During a separation, temporary orders usually involve temporary custody, visitation, financial support of the children, temporary use of property, and servicing of debt. It can include temporary spousal support and the payment of interim attorney's fees as well.

Child custody disputes are often the reason why the divorce process is lengthened. When parents cannot agree on issues related to custody and visitation, additional hearings and proceedings may be required. As stated previously, some states require separation for a required length of time or a waiting period. Some require up to one year and require couples to go through mediation or counseling.

I have seen people who declare that they are getting a divorce and six months later their divorce is final. On the other hand, a friend of mine went through the divorce process for almost three years. The amount of money and time spent was ridiculous. They could not agree on anything. Sadly, the marriage didn't even last a year. Even today, they continue to go to court over custodial and child support issues. Hiring a mediator may have been a better option not to mention a lot less expensive, rather than fighting all of their battles in the courtroom.

My point in talking about how long a divorce can take is to remind you that this is a process. Provided that you and your spouse can be more agreeable than you were in your marriage, the time can be reduced by working together and coming to some agreements. A divorce can take hardly any time at all if a couple agrees on the issues and the divorce is uncontested. For couples seeking to streamline their divorce, the best decision is to hire a mediator and settle every issue prior to filing divorce papers. Participating in mediation saves a great deal of time and gives both parties a sense of fairness because the agreements are created independently.

Despite popular opinion, there is never a good time to go through a divorce. We live in a world of changes, several events at a time. We go from one extreme to another. Life is different from one day to the next and we are continually passing and repassing between conditions of human life. Every time and season is unalterably fixed and determined by God. For it is not in our power to change what is appointed for us.

I am not trying to give you legal advice, but my hope is that you will not spend an outrageous amount of money on attorneys and legal proceedings. The State of Kansas requires parenting classes which encourages a couple to do what is best for their children despite the circumstances. When you can agree to do what's best for your children rather than attacking one another and trying to destroy one another, you and your children will benefit. Divorce coaches are available to help you sort things out at a much more reasonable rate than attorneys.

Seek God's guidance on the selection of an attorney and/or mediator. Pray for your soon to be ex-spouse and yourself that the two of you can work together to dissolve the marriage equitably. The longer you stay in the process the more emotionally drained you will be.

Helpful Scriptures

I am your servant; give me discernment that I may understand your statutes. It is time for you to act, Lord; your law is being broken. Psalms 119:125-126 (NIV)

The Lord said: At the right time, I answered you; on a day of salvation, I helped you. I have guarded you, and given you as a covenant to the people, to restore the land, and to reassign deserted properties. Isaiah 49:8 (CEB)

Without good advice everything goes wrong— it takes careful planning for things to go right.
Proverbs 15:22 (CEV)

The Lord is a safe place for the oppressed—a safe place in difficult times. Psalm 9:9 (CEB)

"And let us not grow weary while doing good, for in due season we shall reap if we do not lose heart."
Galatians 6:9 (NKJV)

"Therefore humble yourselves under the mighty hand of God, that He may exalt you in due time, casting all your care upon Him, for He cares for you."
1 Peter 5: 6-7 (NKJV)

"I waited patiently for the Lord; and He inclined to me, and heard my cry. He also brought me up out of a horrible pit, out of miry clay, and set my feet upon a rock, and established my steps." Psalms 40:1-2 (NKJV)

CHAPTER 12
Divorce is a Life Stressor

Please, LORD, be kind to us! We depend on you. Make us strong each morning, and come to save us when we are in trouble. Isaiah 33:2 (CEV)

HOLMES-RAHE LIFE STRESS INVENTORY

Divorce is stressful, but did you realize it is one of life's most stressful events? In 1967, psychiatrists Thomas Holmes and Richard Rahe examined the medical records of over 5,000 medical patients as a way to determine whether stressful events might cause illnesses. Patients were asked to tally a list of 43 life events based on a relative score. A positive correlation was found between life events and illnesses in those studied. Their results were published as the Social Readjustment Rating Scale (SRRS), known more commonly as the Holmes-Rahe Stress Scale. Other studies have supported the links between stress and illness.

The instructions for the inventory are to review a list of events and check the ones you have experienced in the past 24 months. When I took the stressor scale, I scored positive on the following: divorce, marital separation, change in financial state, change in number of arguments with spouse, trouble with in-laws, change in living conditions, revision in personal habits, change in residence, change in church activities, change in sleeping habits, change in eating habits, and Christmas alone. Divorce alone totaled

73 points which brought my overall score to 371. As soon as I calculated my score, a pop up appeared that read, "Over 300 points: This score indicates a major life crisis and is highly predictive of (80%) of a serious physical illness within the next two years."

I thought I was doing pretty well until I looked at my total score. I'm thankful that I wasn't stricken with a serious illness within that time frame, even though I was diagnosed with Grave's disease related to stressors five years later. I don't have to remind you of the documented relationship between stress and physical illness.

Manage Your Stress

It is important that you get a handle on your stress. Be careful you don't have so many negative events going on in your life that ultimately your score on the stress scale increases. Many of the items I checked on the scale were related to the divorce and appeared out of my control. Yet some were completely within my control. Because I was concerned about my financial situation, I found a higher paying job. Yes, getting a new job shows up on the stress list also, but I welcomed the challenge. I tried to make other positive changes like allowing myself some "me time" and deliberately spending time with people who were supportive. Laughter is great medicine when your life seems upside down, so infusing some fun into your life is important. There were times I could barely find anything to laugh about so I rented the funniest movies I could find just to get a really good laugh.

Prayer in the especially difficult times made a difference for me. I found myself praying several times a day during the darkest times. I can't stress enough that you should have a regular routine when it comes to prayer. I find the morning works better for me because it helps to set the tone for my day. I do my best to pray away all of the things that could possibly come my way. I call it prevention. Other times I find myself praying when I want to say something to someone that I know I shouldn't.

Physical activity is an excellent option for relieving stress. I started taking a yoga class a year ago and wished I had known what I know now. Stretching, breathing, and staying focused during yoga helps me to relax. I have a friend who finds running to be a stress reliever. Exercise will not only make you feel better, it has many other healthful benefits. Find a physical exercise that you enjoy and participate regularly.

Stress is toxic so learn to manage and release stress in your life. If you cannot relieve stress on your own get professional help. In fact, it wouldn't hurt to visit your EAP sponsored through your job, or call a counseling hotline. Hire a coach or a counselor and invest in at least three sessions to see where you are. Go get a massage to help with muscle tightness and pain.

Recently, I studied information on the etiology of cancer. Stress is towards the top of the list. In the last several years, I have prayed for many women who are divorced who have been diagnosed with breast cancer. Sadly, some of them have passed away. Many did not smoke nor did they have a positive family history of cancer. What they all have in common is that they are divorced. Maybe the numbers work out that way. While attending a cancer care leadership training at the Cancer Treatment Centers of America, I learned that 1.7 million people are diagnosed with cancer annually, and one of two men and one out of three women will be diagnosed with some type of cancer in their lifetime. Maybe it is coincidence that one out of two marriages end in divorce. Hmmmm. Something to think about.

Remember, God did not make our bodies to handle prolonged stress. He built in mechanisms for us to handle small bouts of stress. When you find yourself overwhelmed, find a way to release so that you will not do permanent damage to your body, mind, and spirit. Trust in God who will help you bear whatever situations are causing you tension and worry. "Don't worry about anything; instead, pray about everything. Tell God what you need, and thank him for all he has done." (Philippians 4:6 NLT)

Helpful Scriptures

Even young people get tired, then stumble and fall. But those who trust the LORD will find new strength. They will be strong like eagles soaring upward on wings; they will walk and run without getting tired. Isaiah 40:30-31 (CEV)

This is what the LORD says— your Redeemer, the Holy One of Israel: "I am the LORD your God, who teaches you what is best for you, who directs you in the way you should go. If only you had paid attention to my commands, your peace would have been like a river, your well-being like the waves of the sea. Isaiah 48:17-18 (NIV)

But he knows the way that I take; when he has tested me, I will come forth as gold. Job 23:10 (NIV)

When I am afraid, I put my trust in you. In God, whose word I praise— in God I trust and am not afraid. What can mere mortals do to me? Psalms 56:3-4 (NIV)

If you have to go to war, you may find yourselves facing an enemy army that is bigger than yours and that has horses and chariots. But don't be afraid! The LORD your God rescued you from Egypt, and he will help you fight. Before you march into battle, a priest will go to the front of the army and say, "Soldiers of Israel, listen to me! Today when you go into battle, don't be afraid of the enemy, and when you see them, don't panic. The LORD your God will fight alongside you and help you win the battle."
Deuteronomy 20:1-4 (CEV)

Chapter 13
A Thin Line Between Love and Hate

Yes, I hate them—through and through! They've become my enemies too. Psalm 139:22 (CEB)

I remember our solemn wedding vows to love in sickness and in health until death do us part. I confessed my love for my groom to God and all of humanity. I was so in love and there wasn't anything I would not do for him. I even ignored his faults. He was the one for me. Seven years later, love was the last word coming out of my mouth. How did I go from love to hate in a matter of years? How does the person you loved beyond a shadow of a doubt suddenly become your number one archenemy?

Can I say my feelings were actually hate? Maybe hate is too strong of a word. Regardless of the term, I couldn't stand to be around him and I didn't want to hear his voice. I didn't want anyone to mention his name to me. Talking with other women, some of them are comfortable using the hate word to describe their feelings toward their ex. I guess it depends on the situation and what may have led to the relationship going sour.

Even ten years after divorce, some women are still angry and have resentment towards their ex. In an article entitled "Hating the One You Love," author Ben-Zeen argues that the presence of love in a relationship can eventually be a fertile ground for the emergence of hate. He states, "When the intensity and intimacy of love turns sour, hate may be generated. Many crimes have been committed in the name of love" (Ben-Zeen, n.d.).

Interestingly enough we want exclusivity when we love someone; however, when love turns to hate, we want everyone else to hate them as well. We are quick to explain why we feel the way we do to defend our posture. How many times have you found yourself sharing the negative side of the story, leaving out all of the positive aspects? In fact, we can get so used to telling our story and placing the blame on the other person, our mind begins to embellish the story to justify our complaint.

Be careful about using the word hate. In other words, don't go out and buy the "I hate my ex" t-shirt. Yes, believe it or not they sell them on the internet. Please don't spend money to accentuate the hate! Instead get the aggression out of your system in a healthy way. Try writing a letter to your spouse expressing all of your feelings and get it all out. Write the letter by hand as fast as you can, seal it up, and then read it a week later. Do NOT mail the letter. Reading the letter at a later time will help you determine if you are moving forward or if you are still stuck in the same place.
Some recommend performing some type of farewell ritual. Cut up old pictures or burn old love letters or clean your electronic files of pictures, emails, and texts. Pack up all of his or her things that are still in your possession and get rid of them. He or she may appreciate it if you return their items, but that is your choice if the items are still in your possession.

If you have pent up rage, find a healthy way to get a release. Take a kickboxing class or get a gym membership. Find a sport you enjoy playing or find a high intensity exercise that gives you a great workout. If you must hit something, have a boxing match with your pillows so you won't hurt yourself. Lastly, find something positive to focus on instead of hate. Hang around with the people you love. Get a pet or do like my daughter and make regular visits to the pet store to play with the puppies. It's a great stress reliever, because they are so cute and cuddly.

Don't use the word hate; instead, write down the number of things you love. Make a list entitled "The things I love." Write down as many items as you can think of and incorporate the things you love into your daily life until you no longer have the word hate in your vocabulary.

I have met people who hate everything. They hate their job, they hate their neighbors, they hate certain foods, and they hate the weather. Deliver me from people who are so miserable that they hate everything. There is nothing worse than being around someone that detests everything about their life. I had a friend who found something wrong with everything. I finally had to distance myself from her because she could ruin your day just talking about what she ate for breakfast. Make sure you don't become one of those people because no one wants to be around you.

Think about when you have used the word hate in relation to another person. Was it a friend who betrayed you? Was it someone who did something to you that you find hard to forgive? When you used to love someone and now you hate them, you are really saying that you don't care anymore.

Some say the opposite of love is not hate. Blogger Brigid Bishop says, "Hate is not the opposite of love, hate is love in its angriest, ugliest form." (Bishop, 2013) After I read her blog, I understood feelings of hatred a little better. If you really think about it, only those we truly love can cause us to be angry enough to invoke feelings we feel are hatred. However, the Bible teaches us to love and not to hate. Hatred will cause you to focus on what another has done wrong to you and may ultimately lead you to sin. Do the right thing and hate no one, even those who have persecuted you. Look at Jesus' example. He loved the world even when they hated him enough to want him dead.

Helpful Scriptures

You shall not hate your brother in your heart. You shall surely rebuke your neighbor, and not bear sin because of him. Leviticus 19:17 (NKJV)

So Samson's wife broke down in tears before him and said, "You don't love me at all; you hate me, for you have told a riddle to my people and haven't told me the answer!" Judges 14:16 (TLB)

It is better to eat soup with someone you love than steak with someone you hate. Proverbs 15:17 (TLB)

Hatred stirs up trouble; love overlooks the wrongs that others do. Proverbs 10:12 (CEV)

But then Amnon felt intense hatred for her. In fact, his hatred for her was greater than the love he had felt for her. So Amnon told her, "Get out of here!" 2 Samuel 13:15 (CEB)

They have no reason to hate and fight me, yet they do! I love them, but even while I am praying for them, they are trying to destroy me. They return evil for good, and hatred for love. Psalms 109:3-5 (TLB)

I've lived far too long with people who hate peace. I'm for peace, but when I speak, they are for war. Psalms 120:6-7 (CEB)

Chapter 14
The Rumor Mill

So I sent him this reply: "Nothing that you say has happened. You are simply inventing this."
Nehemiah 6:8 (CEB)

The rumors were out of control. I was being accused of all types of sins in addition to being called everything but a child of God. Some said, "She wants to go out and party and can't do that as a pastor's wife." Others said, "She is bored being married to a pastor." Of course others accused one or both of us of being involved in extramarital affairs. A few people made telephone calls to members of our former church in Oklahoma City to get more information about why we had divorced the first time. Some were brave enough to contact our family members or close friends hoping to find out what was going on. Not all of the rumors came back to me, but later I learned of some really ridiculous, fabricated stories.

When you are the topic of vicious gossip, it doesn't feel good. Hearing just a few of the rumors caused me to want to go out and defend myself. Telling my story would be the only way to stop the nasty gossip and false accusations. Once rumors have started, it is too late to defend yourself. After all, the human mind is funny. When people hear rumors, whether they are true or not, the mind convinces the person that the rumor is true. Not to mention, in the crowd's mind, a divorce always has to be somebody's fault. Of course, I had to be the fall girl. After all, my ex-husband was, in their mind, the nicest most humble man on the face of the earth. He couldn't have possibly done anything wrong. Having left the church without a public statement, I was unable to defend myself.

Being a pastor, my ex-husband had no choice but to save face within his congregation and the religious circles he operated in. Therefore, from the pulpit to the entire congregation he made a public statement. I wasn't there but heard about the declaration later on. "Janice and I are getting a divorce. With the main reason being, Janice no longer wants to be a pastor's wife." Unfortunately, only half of the statement was true, but since it came directly from the horse's mouth, it was gospel. Because I was not present and unable to defend myself, other's added to the statement whatever they desired. There were a few individuals brave enough to ask me point blank, but many just shared whatever they heard and then some.

At the time, I was thankful all of the rumors did not come back to me. I am thankful for God's shield and protection during a difficult time. I did not avail myself to hear everything that was said about me, because I chose not to hang around in settings where we had been as a couple. I had to find a church where no one really knew who I was. Of course, I continued to work every day, but the good news was I worked across the state line and very few people at work knew us. On one occasion, a church member visited me at work after being unable to reach me by telephone. I was sitting at my desk when I was informed that I had a visitor. I assumed the visitor was work related and went out to the front desk to see who it was. I was surprised to find a tearful church member inquiring as to why I had left the church and why we were getting divorced. Since our children played together, I was okay with her visit although I didn't share too much information about our pending divorce. I think she just wanted to see my face. After talking for a few moments, I then hugged her and thanked her for her visit and assured her we were going to be okay. I asked her why she came all the way over to visit me. She mentioned calling the house several times and being unable to reach me by phone. Caller ID was a saving grace as I rarely answered the house phone.

I guess our story was really juicy news in our community. We had not been in the community very long, so it was exciting for the locals to have some information about the new kids on the block. The news spread to our former church in Oklahoma City as well. Our situation was the buzz for several months. A few people from Oklahoma City tried to contact me. Once again, thank God for caller ID, because I didn't want to talk to anyone. The question that constantly remained in my head was: why are others so excited to gossip about the lives of others?

Gossip has been around for centuries. People gossiped about Jesus, and especially about the woman at the well, which is why she came to the well to draw water at noonday instead of early in the morning. Often when people feel bad about themselves and their own lives, they feel better when they talk about other's situations. Gossipers also feel important or superior when they are the first to share information or have the inside scoop no one else has. When you are the first person to hear a rumor, you can suddenly become the center of attention.

Most likely you have a few people who are not personal fans of yours, who can't wait to get some negative news about you and will immediately share with others out of jealousy or revenge. Some of the main women who were sharing the gossip were also interested in my ex.

Remember, when someone gossips or shares negative information about you to consider their motivation.

How to Handle Gossip

If you are experiencing separation or divorce, be assured that your situation will pick up much chatter along the way. What can you do when you find yourself the center of gossip? First, make sure you don't start the rumors yourself by sharing the wrong information with the wrong people. Whatever comes out of your mouth will sound totally different by the time it hits the rumor mill. Second, once you hear a rumor has gone out, don't get too emotional. It comes with the territory.

Third, if you happen to ask someone where they heard the rumor, they will most likely give you a name. Please don't start the process of tracking down whoever started a rumor. You will wear yourself out and find yourself ticked off at many people. If you do talk with others, just share the facts and leave the emotion out of it. "Yes, we are getting a divorce and we want to keep this a private matter to protect our children." Whatever you do, don't lie or make up something else to counteract the rumors. Feel free to admit a rumor is false, and be aware people may or may not believe you, so don't spend too much energy denying rumors.

Is complete silence the best solution? I'm not sure because some people see silence as guilt. But trust me, when gossip is involved, you can't win for losing. When I kept my mouth shut, my anxiety sometimes got the best of me and I wanted to shout my story to the entire world in order to defend myself. I decided to let my behavior be my testimony. When the gossipers didn't see me out at the club partying or hanging on the arms of another man, those rumors would have to stop sooner or later. At the same time having a reputable third party speak on your behalf can help your situation. There were a few women who spoke up on my behalf and silenced the blabbermouths who were out to destroy my reputation.

Most of all let your conversation be full of grace. Keep your mouth off others. The last thing you want to do is take attention off yourself by talking about others. Pray and ask for God's guidance on what you should say and how you should say it when you hear the nasty rumors about yourself. Yes, words hurt, but God can not only restore you, but he can deal with those who spread false rumors about you. Don't try to take revenge on others. Let the Lord fight your battles and you will soon be victorious.

Helpful Scriptures

Do not lose heart or be afraid when rumors are heard in the land; one rumor comes this year, another the next, rumors of violence in the land and of ruler against ruler.
Jeremiah 51:46 (NIV)

The LORD said: Don't spread harmful rumors or help a criminal by giving false evidence. Exodus 23:1 (CEV)

His greatest joy will be to obey the LORD. This king won't judge by appearances or listen to rumors. Isaiah 11:3 (CEV)

Don't be a gossip, but never hesitate to speak up in court, especially if your testimony can save someone's life.
Leviticus 19:16 (CEV)

When visitors come, all they ever bring are worthless words, and when they leave, they spread gossip.
Psalm 41:6 (CEV)

Dishonest people use gossip to destroy their neighbors; good people are protected by their own good sense.
Proverbs 11:9 (CEV)

A gossip tells everything, but a true friend will keep a secret. Proverbs 11:13 (CEV)

They cause trouble for people you have already punished; their gossip hurts those you have wounded.
Psalm 69:26 (CEV)

Chapter 15
Divorce and Depression

Why, I ask myself, are you so depressed? Why are you so upset inside? Hope in God! Because I will again give him thanks, my saving presence and my God.
Psalm 42:5 (CEB)

I have heard many times that people who are going through divorce are at risk for depression because divorce is one of the most stressful events a person can experience. Thoughts about the dissolution of your marriage can lead to signs of depression. Left untreated, clinical depression becomes a serious problem and can cause significant problems in relationships and at work. According to Web MD's Depression Health Center, depression is responsible for more than 200 million days lost from work each year. If depression continues to be untreated, the illness can lead to more severe psychological problems, including drug and alcohol addiction.

Untreated depression can also lead to significant health problems including the inability to overcome chronic illnesses. There is more and more evidence that depression takes a serious toll on one's physical health. Untreated depression also carries a risk of suicide. This is the worst but very real outcome of untreated or under-treated depression. Anybody who expresses suicidal thoughts or intentions should be taken very, very seriously.

In the article, *Marital Dissolution and Major Depression in Midlife*, research conducted by the University of Arizona found that divorce has a significant effect on subsequent depression when there is a previous history of depression. Nearly 60 percent of the adults with a history of depression who got divorced experienced a later depressive episode. Compared with those who were still married but had a history of depression, there was only a 10 percent likelihood of another depressive episode (Sbarra et al, 2012).

How do you know if you are depressed? Depression is usually seen in three areas: Psychological/Emotional, Behavioral, and Physical.

Psychological/Emotional
    Feelings of sadness and the inability to say why
    Crying
    Depressed mood
    Low self-confidence
    An indifferent attitude
    Hopelessness
    Suicidal thoughts or recurrent thoughts of death
    Exaggerated feelings of guilt
    Anxiety or feeling scared most of the time

Behavioral
    Indecision
    Inability to control anything
    Self-criticism
    Unrealistic fears leading to inaction
    Reminiscing about the past and trying to recall and relive the days gone past
    Loss of interest or pleasure in activities you used to enjoy
    Difficulty concentrating
    Withdrawal and reclusive behavior
    Lack of desire to do something

Edginess
Inability to problem solve problems due to a fear of failure
Indecisiveness on even trivial issues

Physical symptoms include:
Crying
Sleep disturbance (sleeping more or sleeping less)
Lack of energy and fatigue
Appetite and weight changes

One of the most telling symptoms is a change in sleep patterns. Though the most common problem is insomnia (difficulty getting adequate sleep), people sometimes feel an increased need for sleep and experience excessive lack of energy. A lack of sleep can cause some of the same symptoms as depression—extreme tiredness, loss of energy, and difficulty concentrating or making decisions.

My first depressive-like symptom was sleep disturbances. I was unable to fall asleep at night or I woke up too early in the morning and could not go back to sleep. I tried all the tricks of the trade including going to bed the same time every night, not watching television or reading before getting in the bed, taking a warm shower and drinking chamomile tea. When the first line of self-treatment didn't help I moved up to stronger self-help remedies. When I worked nights, a small dose of the natural supplement melatonin helped me to sleep during the day.

Standing in the sleep aisle at Walgreens, I picked up melatonin, Tylenol PM, and any other over the counter medication to solve my sleep problem. Tylenol PM, which is really a straight antihistamine with acetaminophen, wasn't a good choice. I was extremely drowsy during the day and normal functioning was extremely difficult. Morning grogginess was also a problem with melatonin. My sleeplessness or insomnia caused enough concern for me to mention my struggles during a routine visit with my primary care physician. He recommended sleeping pills until I could get back on track. I tried two prescriptions and finally found one that helped significantly. The meds helped me to fall asleep and stay asleep, but I didn't like the side effects and I was afraid of becoming addicted.

Besides insomnia, I was having difficulty concentrating as so many thoughts were going through my mind. There were so many questions I didn't begin to have answers to. When, where, how, why, and what. I had a bad case of the would haves, should haves, could haves. I thought. "If I had done this or not have done that" we would not be going through a divorce. Work was becoming difficult. I was listening but not hearing when people talked to me.

Appetite and weight changes often occur during depression. Fattening foods could have easily been my comfort, but my ego wouldn't allow me to seek food for the fear of gaining weight. I was not going to gain 20 pounds and give anyone the satisfaction of saying I had packed on the pounds after my marriage broke up. They say looking good is the best revenge, and since I did not seek retribution, I was determined to look good. Instead of gaining weight, I developed irritable bowel syndrome and went back and forth between constipation and diarrhea. Some days I was not hungry at all and had to force myself to eat.

According to Jed Diamond, a men's health expert, depressive symptoms are pretty much the same for women and men, but behavior and thought patterns tend to differ. (Diamond, 2002) Women tend to do the following:

Blame themselves
Feel sad, apathetic, and worthless
Avoid conflicts at all costs
Feel slowed down and nervous
Have trouble setting boundaries
Find it easy to talk about self-doubt and despair
Use food, friends, and "love" to self-medicate

On the other hand, men tend to:
Blame others
Feel angry, irritable, and ego inflated
Feel suspicious and guarded
Create conflicts
Feel restless and agitated
Need to feel in control at all costs
Find it "weak" to admit self-doubt or despair
Use alcohol, TV, sports, and sex to self-medicate

It is essential for you to be aware of signs and symptoms of depression in yourself, your spouse, and/or your children. With the right assistance, depression can be treated before it consumes you. Make a visit to your doctor and discuss your feelings. Your physician may prescribe a combination of medication and counseling. Don't be afraid to seek a mental health professional. Depression is an illness. A professional can assist you and help you to feel better. At the same time, if you notice symptoms in other members of your family, assist them with getting the help they need.

Helpful Scriptures

But God cheers up people in need, and that is what he did when he sent Titus to us. 2 Corinthians 7:6 (CEV)

When Ahab heard this, he tore his clothes and wore sackcloth day and night. He was depressed and refused to eat. 1 Kings 21:27 (CEV)

Have mercy on me, LORD, because I'm depressed. My vision fails because of my grief, as do my spirit and my body. Psalm 31:9 (CEB)

Why, I ask myself, are you so depressed? Why are you so upset inside? Hope in God! Because I will again give him thanks, my saving presence and my God. Psalm 43:5 (CEB)

We are experiencing all kinds of trouble, but we aren't crushed. We are confused, but we aren't depressed. 2 Corinthians 4:8 (CEB)

I can't help but remember and am depressed. Lamentations 3:20 (CEB)

Your anger lasts a little while, but your kindness lasts for a lifetime. At night we may cry, but when morning comes we will celebrate. Psalm 30:5 (CEV)

I put all my hope in the LORD. He leaned down to me; he listened to my cry for help. He lifted me out of the pit of death, out of the mud and filth, and set my feet on solid rock. He steadied my legs. Psalms 40:1-2 (CEB)

This suffering person cried out: the LORD listened and saved him from every trouble. Psalm 34:6 (CEB)

Chapter 16
Change is Inevitable

Produce fruit that shows you have changed your hearts and lives. Matthew 3:8 (CEB)

Change is a part of everyday life, but it takes on a whole new role in divorce. Marriage sounds like a positive change while divorce is immediately viewed as negative. Change can be good or bad, welcomed or rejected, chosen or forced, wanted or unwanted. There are so many adjustments that must be made during a divorce. Most often there are address changes, changes in feelings and emotions, and possibly even a name change. I love the quote by Anatole France,

"All changes, even the most longed for, have their melancholy; for what we leave behind us is a part of ourselves; we must die to one life before we can enter another."

Changes we choose ourselves can tend to be the easiest to make, based on the reason for the adjustment. For instance, consider making a simple change such as deciding to color one's hair. There are several reasons why I may decide to color my hair. Maybe I want to infuse some color for fun by adding hi-lites to my hair. Over the years I have added hi-lites just to give myself a warmer look especially in the summer. On these types of occasions when I want to jazz my look up, the change is a welcome one for me. I smile and readily accept compliments about my new hair color.

In contrast, there have been other occasions when I have discretely gone to the drug store looking for hair color options for covering up gray hair. As I begin to see gray coming around my edges, I have a whole different attitude about coloring my hair. Let me give a little disclaimer, a little bit of gray may not be an issue for some women, but for me it's a sign of getting old that I just refuse to accept. When a few gray hairs appeared, I simply tweezed them out. When the grey hairs multiplied, tweezing was no longer the best option. I was not the least bit excited searching for gray cover-ups or asking my hairdresser about options. In this situation, coloring my hair was no longer a fun experience, but a secret mission to hide signs of aging from the rest of the world. As you can see a decision to color can evoke different responses based on the cause.

I have come to the conclusion that when I choose to change or whether change is inflicted on me, it is still stressful. A history of life throwing unexpected things our way or many sudden fluctuations in our lives can leave us afraid of change. For example, if you have ever been laid off from a job or lost a loved one unexpectedly, change can cause fear. Some changes can never be anticipated; however, there are those we can prepare and brace ourselves for. Here are just a few changes to expect before, during, or after a divorce.

Routine Changes

As a married couple, you develop routines and rituals together and everything rapidly changes as the result of separation and divorce. For instance during divorce two, although my children and I had relocated to a different neighborhood, we made a decision to keep them in the same schools for the remainder of the school year. This decision caused our morning routine to change significantly. Before, I simply got them up in the morning and drove them less than two miles to school. Once we relocated, we had to get up 30 to 45 minutes earlier based on the weather so I could transport them to their schools almost ten miles away. This change drastically altered my route to work. My children were not at all excited about getting up earlier, even though I was making the sacrifice so they didn't have to change schools in the midst of all of the other adjustments we were making.

Name Changes

Some women deliberately include in their divorce papers the right to restore their last name to their maiden name. Others, because of the length of time or due to professional reasons, want to keep their married last name. Since I had children in school, I chose not to change my name. Having the same last name as my children made managing their affairs much easier, especially when travelling. When my children and I vacationed in Mexico, by having the same last name, I didn't have to produce a notarized consent form from my ex-husband indicating it was okay for me to take them out of the country. I did not have to prove that I was their parent because we had the same last name.

Anticipating Changes

When you know change is coming you can plan for it. For instance, I knew I could no longer afford the house we lived in as a family and had to find a new one. Having to move was not a welcomed change for me, but being proactive helped me to feel like I was in control. I had to sit down and plan out my budget and then research places in my price range. By planning everything out, the relocation was much easier to bear. Stop and think about all of the changes you know are coming and begin to plan for them; all the while praying and seeking the Lord's guidance for your life.

Embracing Change

Change always comes bearing gifts. ~ Price Pritchett

In the movie *This Christmas,* the Whitfield family had a tradition of getting together every Christmas. The character played by Loretta Divine found love after her first husband abandoned her. Even though she and her new beau were living together, she didn't feel like her children were ready to accept someone taking the place of their absent father, therefore she did not allow her man to sit at the head of the table. Instead, this void was filled by her eldest son Quentin, played by Idris Elba, who expressed the most opposition regarding their mother having a new man in her life. It wasn't until the end of the movie that Quentin finally accepts the change and symbolically acknowledges his change of heart by allowing Mr. Black to sit at the head of the table. I have seen similar behaviors in my own children who found it difficult to embrace the changes in our lives as the result of divorce. On many occasions my daughter asked if her dad was joining us when we were going on vacation or sometimes if we were going out to eat. I constantly had to remind her of our family changes. When

I remarried and we became a stepfamily, there were many more challenges to embracing change.

Change Yourself

Change Yourself. If you don't like something change it; if you can't change it, change the way you think about it.
~Mary Engelbreit

Even though I didn't want to admit it, there were many things about myself perhaps I needed to change. Some changes were external while many were internal. For instance, my personality and temperament demands order and routine, and I like to be in control at all times. When I say all, I mean all. I created a lot of headaches and trouble in my life by always wanting to be in control. I had to finally accept the truth that I can't control everyone and everything, including myself. Changing one's self may be the hardest change of all, but sometimes our behaviors and attitudes need changing. Real change only comes with a change of heart.

Allow God to change your heart about your most difficult challenges. Maybe God wants you to depend on Him more, maybe He wants you to forgive someone and begin to see them differently. I had to stop seeing my ex-husband as my enemy and think of him as a co-parent. I had to stop complaining about him as a spouse and start thinking about what a great parent he is to our children. Pray for those you want to harm, and watch blessings come your way. Perhaps you are involved in behaviors that are ungodly. Take a long hard look at yourself as seen through God's mirror and make the changes needed in your life.

When we are no longer able to change a situation, we are challenged to change ourselves. ~Viktor Frankl

Change before It is Too Late

I once read a book entitled *Change or Die* by Alan Deutschman. The author concludes that although we all have the ability to change our behavior, we rarely ever do. In his study on the human ability to change, he discusses patients who were suffering from heart problems that were told if they didn't change their behavior and eating habits they would die. Most people changed for a little while and then returned to their old habits, even when their life was at risk. He also discussed the plight of those in the criminal justice system who have been given another chance at life to turn their lives around and yet become repeat offenders. Even companies who were failing because of unsuccessful business practices, when given the opportunity to change, repeated unhealthy behaviors, even though they put their company at risk.

Changing not only requires altering our behavior, but in order to be successful we must change our mindset. Some of our thoughts and behaviors are ingrained into our being and prevent us from being the person God intended us to be. I allowed my beliefs about men based on my own upbringing and relationship with my father to dictate how I viewed them. My experiences taught me to never be dependent on a man and to take care of myself. My independence caused me to be competitive with my husband rather than allowing him to be the head of our household. I knew that in order to be successful in another relationship I was going to have to come face to face with my unhealthy beliefs and attitudes. I am better now, but occasionally find myself wanting to be in control again.

Pray and ask for guidance in those areas of your life you should change and be willing to do the work. Become God's work in progress and watch Him work a miracle in your life. Yes change is hard, but the benefits are worth it. Don't try to change everything at once, but take it one step at a time. Just like those who are suffering from addictions or who are trying to lose weight, often it comes down to mind over matter. Why not employ your Godly resources and get the help you need to make permanent transformations in your life.

Helpful Scriptures

"Change your hearts and lives! Here comes the kingdom of heaven!" Matthew 3:2 (CEB)

Watch yourselves! If your brother or sister sins, warn them to stop. If they change their hearts and lives, forgive them. Luke 17:3 (CEB)

Now change your mind and attitude to God and turn to him so he can cleanse away your sins and send you wonderful times of refreshment from the presence of the Lord. Acts 3:19 (TLB)

God overlooks ignorance of these things in times past, but now directs everyone everywhere to change their hearts and lives. Acts 17:30 (CEB)

Now I'm glad—not because you were sad but because you were made sad enough to change your hearts and lives. 2 Corinthians 7:9 (CEB)

Since you really listened to him and you were taught how the truth is in Jesus, change the former way of life that was part of the person you once were, corrupted by deceitful desires. Ephesians 4:21-22 (CEB)

I correct and discipline those whom I love. So be earnest and change your hearts and lives. Revelation 3:19 (CEB)

Chapter 17
Friend Custody

There are persons for companionship, but then there are friends who are more loyal than family.
Proverbs 18:24 (CEB)

As a married couple you may have other couple friends you fellowship with on a regular basis. Perhaps you invited one another over for dinner or hung out together. Maybe your children are about the same ages and you assist one another with babysitting. We had a few couples we enjoyed spending time with. We hung out on holidays and special occasions such as birthdays, and our children enjoyed playing together.

During a divorce, most assets get divided in half. A couple may decide who gets the property and other belongings, but who gets custody of your friends? Should friends be divided in half? Couple friends are often placed in a delicate position. They care about both of you, but can no longer invite both of you to their house at the same time. Many times women and men want to maintain the friendship separately. What happens the next time they have a party? Should they invite one and not the other? Who decides?

The outcome really depends on who was a friend before your marriage or other conditions surrounding the friendship such as working together or going to church together. The friends I worked with continued to be my friends and if I knew them first or outside of my marriage, they remained friends. Whatever you do, it's not a good idea to try to make people choose. Don't try to influence anyone by bad mouthing your spouse in order to win conflicted friends over to your side.

Your friends should be allowed to decide who they want to maintain as a friend after the divorce. If they suddenly stop returning your calls, don't take it personally. Most of all don't harass them trying to convince them that you are the victim. Don't try to steal friends by confronting them and trying to make them feel sorry for you or guilty for maintaining a relationship with your former spouse.

Some couples can't choose and will continue to invite both of you over which can be extremely awkward. You may have to turn down a few invitations here or there as to not run into your spouse. It gets even more awkward when one or both of you start dating or remarry. Don't be surprised when suddenly the invitations to family and friends' gatherings come to a screeching halt. I remember the first time I didn't get invited to a birthday party for one of my former friends. I had just seen them at the mall and they didn't mention anything. I was really disappointed when I found out the party had already occurred. What was even more disheartening years later was not being invited and finding out my ex-spouse was invited and brought a guest.

Friends often feel like they have to choose between you and your ex-spouse, and they don't know how to continue being friends with both of you during the divorce period. Again, don't take it personally because their choice may have nothing to do with you. Your status may expose their vulnerabilities. Just like they may not have had a clue what was going on in your home, you may not be aware of their marital struggles. Sadly, some of my friends sought my advice later when their marriages were failing or they were going through a divorce themselves.

Some friends will be disturbed because they did not see your divorce coming. You have spent time with them and as far as they were concerned you were as happy as any other couple. Again remember divorce discussions expose vulnerabilities in other marriages. They either say to themselves, *that will never happen to us*, or they are wondering when it will happen to them.

Time to Find New Friends

Stop mourning over old friends and get out there and find some new friends. We often select our friends based on our circumstances. Once I was divorced, I joined the singles group at my church. Some people view the singles group as a place to go and find a new mate, but I viewed my participation in the group as an opportunity to make friends with those who shared similar experiences with me. We had a lot of variety in our group including the young and never married and those who had been married previously. Some of the members of our group were actively seeking a mate which explains why one gentleman asked every woman in the group out for a date. We finally figured out his tactics and warned the new ones to the group. Poor guy, he was desperately trying to find a new wife. At least he was trying to find one at church.

When speaking with the never married, I consistently encouraged them to find someone, but to make sure they were selecting the right one before jumping into marriage. I didn't want them to end up divorced like me. Then there were the newly divorced like me and some were still hurting and struggling in their new status. I felt the need to minister to them also, because I wanted to encourage them that God still loved them. Finally, there were also those who were comfortable with being single, regardless of why they were single. I considered them the "Single and Satisfied" group. They had learned to be content in whatever circumstances they were in. I was proud when I finally became a member of the single and satisfied group. Hopefully, you will arrive there at some point.

Use Godly discernment when seeking new friends. Pray for guidance and God will send the right people your way. Be careful of those who just want to get the real story. Be careful of finding pity party buddies. Seek out friends who are like-minded who also share your values. The quickest way to ruin your testimony is to choose the wrong friends. Choose your friends wisely.

Friends can come from anywhere. Many of my post-divorce friends were heaven sent. One of my dearest friends is Tina. My daughter and her granddaughter were best friends in elementary school. She often brought her granddaughter over or we hung out as a foursome. We met at church and she was a big help for me.

One morning I was at a breakfast meeting at the State Capitol and met a woman named Bev that I really admired for her business acumen. We exchanged numbers but never contacted one another because she lived in Wichita which was about three hours from me. As fate would have it we met again two years later at a planning session and immediately recognized one another. We finally had a chance to share and realized we had so many things in common. We both were previously married to pastors, and were now remarried with stepchildren. It was amazing how our lives had taken similar paths. Bev has become one of my closest and best friends.

FRIENDS OF THE OPPOSITE SEX

It is okay to have friends of the opposite sex during this time frame, but walk carefully. A friend may come out of the woodwork, confessing their love for you, but refrain from getting involved romantically with anyone for at least a year after your divorce is final. The optimal time is two years. Clearly define the friendship. Their marital status may also determine if you can be friends or remain friends.

Finally, it's too bad you can't keep all of your friends after a divorce, but it is reality. There's a time for everything and friends were meant to be in your life for a season. Now that you are in a new season, it is time for new friends. Friends can be helpful in this difficult season in your life and they can be found in many places even if you have known them for a long time. There are some old friends who will stick by you and support you and you can always count on them through thick and thin. They may have been there for you before you married and will continue to be your friend.

Be careful of those who unexpectedly appear, wanting to get the scoop rather than truly befriending you. Stay away from those who only want to hear the drama. If they are calling you every day to find out what's going on, they may be more addicted to your drama than to being your friend. Stop feeding them. As times and circumstances change, so do friends. Take an inventory of your friends and decide which ones you want to remain your friends. Be social and friendly; but choose your post-divorce friends carefully. Remember your first day of school? You were nervous about making friends, yet by end of the week you had at least two best friends.

Helpful Scriptures

I choose as my friends everyone who worships you and follows your teachings. Psalm 119:63 (CEV)

We are often troubled, but not crushed; sometimes in doubt, but never in despair; there are many enemies, but we are never without a friend; and though badly hurt at times, we are not destroyed. 2 Corinthians 4:8-9 (GNT)

My enemies are not the ones who sneer and make fun. I could put up with that or even hide from them. But it was my closest friend, the one I trusted most. We enjoyed being together, and we went with others to your house, our God. Psalms 55:12-14 (CEV)

You have made my friends turn in horror from me. I am a prisoner who cannot escape. Psalm 88:8 (CEV)

Each night, bitter tears flood her cheeks. None of her former lovers are there to offer comfort; her friends have betrayed her and are now her enemies. Lamentations 1:2 (CEV)

My friends scorn me, but my eye pours out tears to God. Job 16:20 (AMP)

My best friends and loved ones have turned from me. Job 19:19 (CEV)

CHAPTER 18
Letting Others Down

*I trust you, Lord God, and you will do something. I said,
"Don't let them laugh or brag because I slip."*
Psalms 38:15-16 (CEV)

I said I would never get a divorce. I stood before God and man and said my wedding vows to stay married until "death do us part." Now, I imagined what was going through the minds of those who attended our wedding and perhaps those who said the marriage wouldn't last. We were a ministry couple and supposed to set the example for the other couples in the church. Is it not the first family's duty to present themselves as the happiest couple in the church? After all, didn't others desire to pattern their marriage after the pastor and wife? Even if they are not happy, they were supposed to at least stay together for the sake of everyone else, right? How could the pastor and wife help someone else, yet they couldn't help themselves?

Believe it or not, there were times I was more concerned about my ex-husband's ministry than I was my own reputation. How was he going to be able to counsel married couples or those considering or planning marriage? Would his congregation feel like he was no longer capable of being a minister or a pastor? Would our divorce ruin his chances of being an effective leader? Because I was concerned for him, I deliberately kept my mouth shut about our marital problems and what had led to our divorce.

As the pastor's wife I was involved in several ministries in the church. Teaching Sunday school was my favorite activity as well as working with the women. On occasions, I was requested by local, district, and state church associations for speaking engagements. I loved working with the new members as a spiritual counselor helping them in their transition to a new church. Of course my primary role was being the supportive wife of a Godly man who was trying to build his ministry. Was getting a divorce going to ruin my testimony? Was I going to be asked to step down from the leadership roles I held? In divorce one, I remained at the same church as my ex. Just about the time we announced we were getting a divorce, I was scheduled to speak with a group of missionary ladies. My ex suggested I decline the speaking engagement. I did. Looking back, I cancelled because I somehow felt unworthy of being able to teach anyone else.

During divorce two, I left the church and found another church as far away as possible hoping no one would recognize me as the woman who left her husband and the church. In addition to being concerned for my ex-husband's ministry, I wanted my children to be able to adjust to a new church. On the recommendation of my ex-husband, I found a small church in a small community about twenty miles away from his church. Once I joined, which was a very emotional process, I began to assist with the youth ministry as a Sunday school teacher and other Christian education activities involving my children. What were people going to think of me when they found out I was divorcing a pastor? Were they going to request that I not be allowed to work with their children? Were parents going to remove their children from my Sunday school class? In my mind I imagined the worst case scenario which included being asked to leave the church. Fortunately, my new church members embraced me and were delighted I wanted to teach Sunday school and work with the youth.

Disappointing Family

Another struggle for me was feeling like I had let my family down. I wanted my parents to be proud of me and I know my mom valued my being married to a minister. I was a third generation minister's wife on my mother's side and she had a sense of pride of having two daughters married to ministers. As the granddaughter of a minister, Mom learned at a very young age the importance of working and serving in the church. She was very involved in church mission activities and widely known in religious circles. When introducing me to others she said, "This is my daughter, Janice. She is the one married to the minister." She always said those words with such pride.

I was apprehensive of telling Mom I was getting a divorce the first time and even more troubled announcing the divorce the second time. I was hoping that my sister being married to a pastor would be consolation for her. Again, my own irrational thoughts were totally ridiculous. I imagined my mother being extremely disappointed and angry with me. When Mom and I finally discussed my situation, of course her love was unconditional. She reminded me that I didn't have to endure the things she did as a wife. She said, "You are more than capable of taking care of yourself without having a husband." I was relieved she did not judge me or make me feel worse. I was so grateful for Mom's love and understanding. My Dad didn't have any comments. Well, actually I can't remember having a conversation with him. Thankfully Mom shared everything with him. My sisters were supportive as all of them had been married and had their own struggles.

In general, being in public venues where we were used to being a couple was stressful. Once we were separated, we were required to update the school records and change address information. I had to list two addresses instead of one and complete the box labeled "Additional Household." I'm sure school secretaries receive change forms almost daily, but I still felt like I was disappointing my children's teachers who had complemented us on raising such wonderful children.

Facing other parents at school or sporting events wasn't the least bit pleasurable. Even though we were separated or divorced, my ex and I continued to attend parent teacher conferences and sporting events together to show a united front for our children. I believe our behavior reduced the amount of gossip amongst the "soccer moms." Even when we remarried or began dating other individuals, we sat together at sporting events, school plays, and other activities our children were involved in.

Causing Others to Stumble

Somehow, when divorce happens to what appears to be the perfect couple, other people's vulnerabilities are exposed. Once our announcement was made, a few women commented to me that they were frightened. "If it can happen to you and your husband, what are our chances?" A few even commented that they would have never guessed that divorce could happen to us. "We looked up to you guys and patterned our marriages after you."

Even more heartbreaking is feeling like your divorce is the catalyst for the dissolution of other's marriages. Just hearing of another couple calling it quits made me feel like it was my fault. What was even more disheartening was when I received phone calls from women who wanted my advice on leaving their husbands. In their mind, I had faired very well and they wanted to know how I did it. I was a "shero" in their eyes. They usually left disappointed as I strongly encouraged them to stay in their marriages.

Having to face others really affected my confidence level. I could have easily become a hermit, but life must go on. I found myself praying for confidence every time I left the house for a public venue where others had recently learned of my new status. After a few months, being amongst others became easier. I gradually stopped all of the negative self-talk wondering what others were thinking or saying about me. I had to ask myself, "Who was I trying to please or impress anyway?"

My prayers were answered and I began to accept that other's failed marriages were not my fault. Couples were divorcing before I got divorced and more were going to go through marital difficulties and their situations had nothing to do with me. In addition, there were people talking about me when I was married, so what was the difference? There will always be the negative ones who have nothing good to say about anyone.

Why was I so worried about disappointing people? The one I should have been most concerned about was God. What did He think of me? Was He angry with me? Joyce Meyers wrote a book entitled *God is Not Mad at You*. What a blessing her book has been to me and to others whom I have recommended to read it.

The Bible instructs us that God loves us unconditionally and there's nothing we can do that His grace and mercy will not cover. I kept reading the scripture Psalm 118:6 (CEV): "The Lord is on my side, and I am not afraid of what others can do to me."

Slowly my confidence was restored. I was no longer ashamed to be around people and worried about what they thought of me. Trust me, people have enough issues of their own, so why are they looking at the splinter in my eye, when they have a telephone pole sticking out of theirs? Yes, God is disappointed when we divorce, but he still loves us. We are still the same person He created and His love and peace will be with us despite our marital status.

Helpful Scriptures

But the Lord said to Moses and Aaron, "Because you refused to believe in my power, these people did not respect me. And so, you will not be the ones to lead them into the land I have promised." Numbers 20:12 (CEV)

I know about my sins, and I cannot forget my terrible guilt. Psalm 51:3 (CEV)

Don't judge by appearances. Judge by what is right. John 7:24 (CEV)

"In the fear of the LORD there is strong confidence, and His children will have a place of refuge." Proverbs 14:26 (NKJV)

"Don't put your confidence in powerful people; there is no help for you there." Psalm 146:3 (NLT)

"Beloved, if our heart does not condemn us, we have confidence toward God." 1 John 3:21 (NKJV)

"For the LORD will be your confidence, and will keep your foot from being caught." Proverbs 3:26 (NKJV)

Don't fall in love with money. Be satisfied with what you have. The Lord has promised that he will not leave us or desert us. That should make you feel like saying, "The Lord helps me! Why should I be afraid of what people can do to me?" Hebrews 13:5-6 (CEV)

CHAPTER 19
Loneliness

My God! My God, why have you left me all alone? Why are you so far from saving me, so far from my anguished groans? Psalms 22:1-2 (CEB)

Divorce is like taking a whole and cutting it in half. The person who slept next to you in the bed for many years, the person you shared your life with, the person you shared your love with, and the person you shared your dreams with, is now detached from you. Something is definitely missing in your life. Even if you were arguing all the time, and are glad to have the peace and quiet, you may still feel lonely.

What does it feel like to be lonely? There is nothing pleasant about feeling lonely. Loneliness is how we respond emotionally to isolation or a lack of companionship. Even when you are in a crowd of people, you may still feel alone. Many married people have complained of feeling alone even while married and living in the house with several people. Having more social connections is not necessarily the answer when you are dealing with loneliness as the result of a divorce. You may feel lonely, but may not feel up to being around others.

The times I did feel lonely were usually around holidays. For instance, if the visitation schedule caused the children to be with their father on Christmas day, it was strange waking up on Christmas morning alone. My ex and I worked out an arrangement on Christmas day to alert one another when the children were awake and then either of us would drive across town to be there when our children opened their gifts. We continued the tradition of both of us being there for our children on Christmas until I remarried. When our daughter was young we were still trying to convince her that Santa would visit her no matter what house she was at.

One of the most difficult adjustments for me whenever my children were not present was eating alone. In my children's absence, I didn't sit at the traditional dining room table. Instead, I ate in the den perhaps in front of the television. When my children were not present, I made it a point to cook foods like asparagus and other vegetables my children didn't like to eat. Having an opportunity to enjoy some of my favorite foods helped to make dining alone somewhat of a treat. Eating out was a different story. Looking at everyone else eating as a couple or a family was uncomfortable for me, so often I purchased my meals to go. I didn't understand why eating out was difficult, as I often dined alone when I went on business trips. Maybe I was concerned about running into someone I knew. If I did go out and eat, I would take work with me or a book in order to appear preoccupied.

Home Alone

During the weekends when my children were with their father, I planned my weekend with activities I enjoyed. My activities did not necessarily include being around people. Sometimes I stopped by the library or the bookstore on Thursday and picked up a book I wanted to read. I took advantage of the silence and took a hot bubble bath or a much needed nap. Sometimes I wrote in my journal, other times I did research on the internet. My sister tried to get me to go into chat rooms with her, but the first time a guy tried to pick me up on the internet by asking my pantyhose size, I knew chat rooms were not for me. This is of course before Facebook became popular among people my age.

Soon I began to look forward to the weekends that my children were gone. I stayed home by myself and only went out to go to the grocery store and to church on Sunday mornings. On occasion I invited other single girlfriends over for a cook-out, or we went to the movies or out to eat. I actually enjoyed the quiet time and didn't really think about loneliness. Being home alone was just what the doctor ordered. My favorite pastime during the difficult times was reading. I always had a book on hand. Whenever the weather was warm enough, local parks or lakes were my chosen spots to just sit for hours and read. During the winter months, I found my favorite, warm, fuzzy robe and curled up in a chair by my imagined fireplace and lost myself in books the entire weekend with the exception of church on Sundays.

As I began to establish my new life as a single, I made friends with other single women at the church I attended. We did things like going out to dinner and to the movies or shopping. Many of us were involved in the singles ministry and we attended planned outings or went to monthly single's ministry meetings.

It is very common for persons going through a divorce to experience loneliness. The loss of a relationship and not communicating with that person on a regular basis may leave you longing for the other person to be around. You may miss being in certain circles with the person and no longer have social events to attend. Establish new routines and learn to appreciate being by yourself. You may feel awkward in the beginning, but start by doing things you enjoy doing alone. If a quiet environment bothers you, play music or turn the television on for background noise. Spend time outside in nature and surround yourself with all that God has created for our enjoyment. Remember, Jesus' words; "He will never leave us nor forsake us."

Helpful Scriptures

But so many people were coming and going that Jesus and the apostles did not even have a chance to eat. Then Jesus said, "Let's go to a place where we can be alone and get some rest." Mark 6:31 (CEV)

But Jesus would often go to some place where he could be alone and pray. Luke 5:16 (CEV)

Turn to me, God, and have mercy on me because I'm alone and suffering. Psalm 25:16 (CEB)

Even if my father and mother should desert me, you will take care of me. Psalm 27:10 (CEV)

Don't leave me all alone, Lord! Please, my God, don't be far from me! Psalm 38:21 (CEB)

The Lord loves justice. He will never leave his faithful all alone. They are guarded forever, but the children of the wicked are eliminated. Psalm 37:28 (CEB)

I lie awake all night. I'm all alone like a bird on a roof. Psalm 102:7 (CEB)

Also, if two lie down together, they can stay warm. But how can anyone stay warm alone? Ecclesiastes 4:11 (CEB)

Chapter 20
Money, Money, Money

If you love money and wealth, you will never be satisfied with what you have. This doesn't make sense either.
Ecclesiastes 5:10 (CEV)

Money can definitely be a source of contention while going through a divorce. If financial matters are the number one reason couples divorce, splitting up doesn't improve financial disputes. Before it's all over, you may have several disagreements about how to divide and distribute your money. Each person may feel like they will not have enough, so will fight hard for their financial protection. One of the consequences of divorce is that some women and children are left living in poverty. Sometimes women in particular suffer, because they are most often not the family breadwinner. Here are some common areas you must concern yourself with.

Not Enough Money

If you were having financial troubles before the divorce, your financial problems will be magnified. The same amount of money that was contributing to one household now has to support two homes. Now there are two rent payments, two electricity payments and other household expenses. You may be in a position where you are unable to support yourself and or your family on your salary alone. Perhaps you are paying child support and there is not enough money left over to pay your car insurance. For others, even with receiving child support and /or alimony, money is still tight and you struggle to pay for your children's lunches. You may have to make some really tough choices. Once I began to make plans for where my children and I would live, I knew I had to make some changes. I had to bring in additional income or find an inexpensive apartment. I decided to increase my income as there were no more expenses to cut. I began looking for a job with a higher salary in order to make ends meet.

Child Support

Most often if children are involved, the non-custodial parent will be required to pay the custodial parent a determined amount of money for child support. Over the years I have found the average to be around $350 a month per child. At the same time, I have seen custodial parents get a whole lot more and some get a whole lot less. The divorce decree will determine how much and when the money should be paid. Usually child support is paid at the beginning of the month, but I have seen money taken out per pay period and paid in two monthly installments.

In the state of Kansas where I reside, child support had to be paid through a payment processing center and then the amount was deposited into my account. Once child support is awarded, it has to be paid until the child turns eighteen and graduates from high school. Amounts are not necessarily permanent. If significant financial changes occur in either's lives, the couple may return to court to increase or decrease amounts. Failure to pay child support can lead to criminal charges including jail time, if charges are filed for nonpayment.

Alimony

Some women I knew who did not work outside the home or only worked part-time filed for alimony in addition to child support. Spousal alimony or support is the payment from one spouse to another, often to make up for the reduced financial resources of the receiving spouse, or to compensate for that spouse's contribution to the home or the other spouse's career advancement.

How much is a typical alimony payment? There is no set amount. It's based on several financial components including salary, assets, debts, as well as considerations such as one spouse supporting another through school or starting a business, or one spouse being a homemaker. Either spouse can file for alimony. Alimony is usually temporary, maybe five to ten years, but in some cases it may be permanent. Alimony is a big deal if one of the spouses has a high income such as that of professional athletes and actors and actresses. There is always a sports figure or someone in Hollywood getting divorced or forced to pay child support or alimony at extravagant amounts. More and more couples are signing pre-nuptial agreements to prevent the other person from requesting huge monthly or one-time payments. My ex and I were making approximately the same amount of money so I did not file for alimony; however, I know others who received maintenance payments from their former spouses.

A Whole Minus Half is Less than Half

When separating, a complete household is now a divided household and either one or both persons must relocate from the original dwelling place. In our first divorce, my ex-husband moved in with his brother for a few weeks until he was able to lease an apartment. My son and I continued to live in the three bedroom home we had purchased four years prior. Remaining in the house allowed me to keep life as normal as possible for our son. Eventually we sold the house and I was able to buy a smaller house in a neighborhood where there were many children for him to play with.

During our second divorce we owned a much more expensive home and neither one of us would have been able to make the payments alone. Therefore, I resided in the master bedroom on the second floor and he moved downstairs two levels to the finished basement. The lower level was equipped with all the basics for a small apartment with the exception of a kitchen. Once our house was on the market, we were fortunate to find a buyer within two weeks, resulting in a decent profit for both of us. We split the proceeds and had enough money to easily set up separate residences. We had only been in the house for two years so we were thankful for coming out of it with a profit rather than a loss.

About six months before our divorce, my ex-husband left his vice-president position to become a full-time pastor. Without his corporate salary our annual incomes were roughly the same; therefore, when our divorce financial documents were calculated, we were responsible for the same amount of financial support for our children. In other words, I wasn't getting a lot of child support. Keeping up our standard of living was going to be tough on my salary alone.

In our first divorce, I had a management job and we lived in Oklahoma which did not have a very high cost of living. With a basic amount of child support per month, my son and I did well. I purchased a three-bedroom home with a two car garage in a nice neighborhood. Divorce two, occurred in Johnson County Kansas which is one of the richest counties in the nation with a much higher cost of living than Oklahoma. Housing prices were almost double and sometimes triple what we paid for a home in Oklahoma. Everything was more expensive including the price of gas, food, and even hair appointments.

As I began to look at my future budget, fear set in. I realized money was going to be really tight. In looking for a new place to live, I viewed luxury apartments, town homes, and duplexes mainly because I could not stand the thought of not having a garage and having to scrape my car during the cold Kansas winters. As I looked at my future budget, I realized I was going to need more money. One thought was to increase the amount of child support. As previously mentioned, the standard rate for child support loomed around $350 per child per month and we had two children. An extra $700 a month was great, but a thousand would be better. When the time came around to set the amount with my attorney, I ended up putting down the standard amount. Knowing my ex was no longer working as the vice president at the bank, I knew he was going to struggle financially. I knew I was being nice by not asking for more than the standard; however, I still needed more money.

Instead, I prayed for guidance which led me to look for a job that paid more money. God answered my prayers and it didn't take long to find a higher paying job. The increase in salary allowed me the opportunity to purchase a house so we could get out of the smaller townhouse. There was enough money to travel and afford the simple things we enjoyed, like eating out and shopping.

Bank Accounts

When my husband and I split, we opened individual accounts, but failed to close the joint account. Soon I got a bill in the mail to cover the monthly service fees. We had left about fifty dollars in the account and forgotten about it. Six to eight months later when the fees had eaten up the balance the bank was forced to close the account because of the negative balance. Because he had moved his account to another bank, I was responsible for the additional fees and was not happy about it.

Families have different practices when it comes to finances. Both may manage the bank account and bills or only one person is responsible for money matters. In our case we had joint accounts with separate checkbooks and visa check cards. If you have joint accounts, it's a good idea to go to the bank together to close your current accounts. This should not be done in the absence of the other person. As soon as possible determine how to divide what is currently in your joint bank accounts. Remember, if you are still in the household there are bills to pay. As soon as possible, set up separate checking accounts and deposit your next payroll check into the new account.

Money Worries

Fear of not having enough may compel you to hoard money before your spouse does. Stories have been told of spouses who clear out the bank accounts leaving the other with just a few dollars. I hear all the time from women that others have suggested they always keep a small bank account of their own just in case their husband leaves them. They secretly skim money off of the joint account to protect themselves. Do not secretly clean out the account. I know emotions are high, but you don't want to get into a money fight.

I am aware that some women do not work or have their own money, nor are all women on equal footing financially with their spouses as I was. As soon as possible, sit down and have a discussion about how you will divide your assets. Don't forget to have a discussion about joint debt. Discuss how children will be provided for. Some couples are unable to have a financial discussion without the intervention of their attorneys or a mediator. Determine whether or not you will need additional help and get these matters solved as quickly as possible.

My views on money may be different than some. Somehow, watching my mom being financially dependent on my father caused me to have the attitude that I was not going to depend on a man to take care of me. Having this belief while going through a divorce served me well. I had the confidence that God was going to provide. I knew He would provide me with the blessing of a higher paying job or other opportunities to increase my income. I was not going to sit around waiting on the child support check every month and not try to do something myself to improve my situation.

God opened so many doors. I had never done consulting work in my life, but God opened some doors for me to make additional money. I could not believe that someone would pay me $250 to sit in on a conference call or over a thousand dollars just to read, review, and discuss grant applications. I saved a lot of money by not shopping. In fact, I sold some of my clothes to resale shops or signed with consignment stores. My income tax checks were bigger because I filed as the head of household. God was always full of surprises and I feel like I was blessed beyond measure. I have to believe that my blessing came because I did not try to destroy my ex financially.

Some of you may not have been a bread winner and your spouse worked while you stayed at home. Your situation is much different and you may have to fight for everything you get. Pray and ask the Lord for guidance and get yourself a really good lawyer. You may also want to hire a divorce coach to help you to determine your financial future. If you suspect your ex is hiding money or property, a good attorney can assist you.

Helpful Scriptures

I know what it is to be poor or to have plenty, and I have lived under all kinds of conditions. I know what it means to be full or to be hungry, to have too much or too little. Christ gives me the strength to face anything.
Philippians 4:12-13 (CEV)

If you love money and wealth, you will never be satisfied with what you have. This doesn't make sense either.
Ecclesiastes 5:10 (CEV)

God may give some people plenty of wealth, riches, and glory so that they lack nothing they desire. But God doesn't enable them to enjoy it; instead, a stranger enjoys it. This is pointless and a sickening tragedy.
Ecclesiastes 6:2 (CEB)

It's better to enjoy what's at hand than to have an insatiable appetite. This too is pointless, just wind chasing.
Ecclesiastes 6:9 (CEB)

"If one of you wanted to build a tower, wouldn't you first sit down and calculate the cost, to determine whether you have enough money to complete it? Luke 14:28 (CEB)

The wealthy rule over the poor; a borrower is a slave to a lender. Proverbs 22:7 (CEB)

CHAPTER 21
Outrage and Anger

My dear friends, you should be quick to listen and slow to speak or to get angry. If you are angry, you cannot do any of the good things that God wants done. James 1:19-20 (CEV)

I'm Angry

We all remember the scene in the movie *Waiting to Exhale* when Angela Bassett's character, Bernadine, gathers all of her husband's things out of the closet, loads his belongings in a little red wagon, throws everything in his car, backs the car out of the garage, opens the sun roof, douses it with lighter fluid, sets it on fire, lights a cigarette, watches the car burn, then flicks her cigarette, and walks away. If you don't remember how intense the scene was check it out on YouTube (Bernadine's Rage). Oh, I forgot to mention, she does all of this while wearing a sexy negligée. She obviously feels justified once she has destroyed his belongings. I remember sitting in the movie clapping with other women celebrating Bernadine's victory in getting it all out. Her final comment to the policeman who discovered the fire was, "Don't worry, it won't happen again."

Allow me to refresh your memory in another scene where a scorned woman shares her frustrations. In a scene from the movie *Diary of a Mad Black Woman,* Helen, played by Kimberly Elise, makes the statement, "I'm not bitter, I'm mad as hell." Better yet, remember when Madea instructs Helen on how to destroy the other woman's clothes?

Madea: "Rip it real good. Rip it!"

Helen says, "Wait a minute. What is this going to solve?"

Madea: "Nothing. It's just gonna make you feel better."

Somewhere along the way you may become angry. I can't say when it will come for you but it will. Just about anything can set you off—hearing a rumor; discovering there is not enough money in the bank, or hearing your children mention Dad or Mom's new friend. You could be like Bernadine and get angry when you feel like you have wasted the last ten to twenty years of your life. Maybe he or she took the money and ran. Maybe it's someone else. Maybe it's something he or she said.

People respond to anger differently. My daughter and current husband both tell me they know when I am angry by the way I hold my mouth. My husband calls it "pressing my lips." According to them my mouth reveals it all. Being a pastor's wife, I have probably perfected being able to hold my emotions to a minimum in public. However, the older I get the more challenging it is to control my facial expressions. I don't get angry easily, but when I finally allow everything to build up, fury begins to slowly rise through my body until I feel like I want to explode. My only release when I get to this point is to have a private painful crying episode. It doesn't last very long, and once it's over I feel somewhat better even though I look a hot mess from crying.

Your Body and Anger

Anger can be expressed in many ways. Physiological behavior may include teeth grinding, fist clenching, flushing, turning pale, sweating, temperature changes, and muscle tension. When I am angry I can feel the tension in my body. My shoulders tighten and I get hot flashes. On occasion when I go to bed angry, I usually wake up with a headache. I wonder if I am grinding my teeth.

From a scientific point of view, let's consider what happens in our brains when we become angry. I learned in graduate school that when our brain experiences the emotion of anger, the amygdale, the part of the brain that deals with emotion, goes crazy and wants to do something immediately. It wants to wreak havoc and attack whatever has caused the anger. This happens in a quarter of a second. To protect us from doing something too crazy right away blood flows to the frontal lobe which is the part of the brain that controls reasoning. We are grateful for the front part of our brain for taking over and keeping us from destroying ourselves or others. These two areas of the brain quickly balance out one another. You may have heard that if you are really angry you should count to ten. Taking a pause gives the frontal part of the brain time to kick in to keep you from doing harm to yourself or others.

Numerous studies have been designed to research the long term effects of anger. In an article by Molly Edmonds entitled "How Anger Works," she reviews the many aspects of anger. What caught my eye was the damage that this emotion can do to our bodies. Anger increases our risk for chronic diseases like coronary artery disease and heart attacks, even breast cancer. She mentioned that some scientists consider chronic anger to be more dangerous to the body than smoking and obesity. I have seen this phenomena occur where individuals harbor anger and unforgiveness and as a result the anger eventually manifested itself in the form of a deadly illness.

You've seen it happen. You get angry and want to do physical harm to someone. Do you remember the scene in *Fried Green Tomatoes* when the character played by Kathy Bates is riding through the parking lot of the Winn Dixie grocery store looking for a parking space? She is minding her own business, driving through the grocery store parking lot singing, "If I can help somebody as I pass along," the gospel version mind you, indicating she is prayed up. When the young girls steal her parking spot, Kathy becomes angry. She starts repeating the word "Towanda" and the church music turns into something else as she continuously rams into the back of the Volkswagen with her big car. I can't remember how many times that scene has flashed in my mind looking for parking spaces in the mall or at Wal-Mart.

Just about everybody in the family will become angry sometime during the divorce process. You will be angry at your spouse and he or she will most likely be angry at you. Your children will probably be angry at one or both parents for ruining their lives. Everyone may blame the other for the demise of the family. Children may even blame themselves.

Learn how to deal with your anger in a healthy way. To express your anger, write a letter or punch a pillow if you have to. Recognize anger immediately and deal with it. Here are some practical suggestions for dealing with your irritation:

1. Be angry and sin not. Most of all keep your mouth shut until you can speak without causing permanent damage.
2. Step away from the situation for a moment. Try counting to ten or to a hundred if you have to. Give the front part of your brain time to kick in and think about the situation. Take a few deep breaths while you are pulling yourself together.
3. Make the decision that you are not going to allow others to control your emotions. Don't let them push your buttons. Plan in advance next time not to go there with them.
4. Start praying and smile because God's got your back.
5. Stay away from any items you can use to inflict harm on another or damage another's property. Don't do anything that can land you in jail.

Helpful Scriptures

When I heard their complaints and their charges, I became very angry. Nehemiah 5:6 (CEV)

It upset me so much that I threw out every bit of Tobiah's furniture. Then I ordered the room to be cleaned and the temple utensils, the grain offerings, and the incense to be brought back into the room. Nehemiah 13:8-9 (CEV)

A hot-tempered man starts fights and gets into all kinds of trouble. Proverbs 29:22 (TLB)

Only fools get angry quickly and hold a grudge. Ecclesiastes 7:9 (CEV)

I'm not angry, but if it yields thorns and thistles for me, I will march to battle against it; I will torch it completely. Isaiah 27:4 (CEB)

But I say to you that everyone who is angry with their brother or sister will be in danger of judgment. Therefore, if you bring your gift to the altar and there remember that your brother or sister has something against you, leave your gift at the altar and go. First make things right with your brother or sister and then come back and offer your gift. Matthew 5:22 & 24 (CEB)

Don't get so angry that you sin. Don't go to bed angry. Ephesians 4:26 (CEV)

Chapter 22
Resentment

Resentment kills a fool, and envy slays the simple.
   Job 5:2 (NIV)

"Resentment is like taking poison and waiting for the other person to die." ~ Malachy McCourt

We often feel resentful when someone has offended us and may find it hard to forgive that person. Resentment, also known as bitterness, can often result after the divorce process. The ex may do and say things that become ingrained in your memory forever. We may play those tapes over and over in our minds leading to more ill feelings. Before long, we add more fuel to the fire until bitterness arrives. Consider the following definitions from Dictionary.com:

> **ANGER:** a strong feeling of displeasure and belligerence aroused by a wrong.
> **RESENTMENT:** the feeling of displeasure or indignation at some act, remark, person, etc., regarded as causing injury or insult.
> **BITTERNESS:** difficult to accept: mentally painful, or very hard to accept.

Once emotions run high, anger, resentment and bitterness may all appear the same. Recall another scene from the movie, *Diary of a Mad Black Woman*, Kimberly

Elise's character (Helen) makes the statement, "I'm not bitter, I'm mad as hell!" When our anger gets to this point it can easily lead to resentment. Somewhere our anger goes bad and turns into something we can't seem to control. If left unresolved, resentment has the power to distort our view of the world and the persons we resent.

Resentment usually harms the one who resents more than it does the one who is resented. With so much internalized anger, one's behavior can become abusive or self-destructive.

Having a conversation with a co-worker one day and realizing how much she was getting in child support, caused me to be resentful of my ex. I felt like I had been robbed. Some women were getting twice the amount from their exes, than I was receiving from mine. The more I dwelt on it, the angrier I became. I started thinking about taking him back to court or sending him a list of items I thought he should pay for. I stewed whenever he bought a new car or when the kids told me he always had a wad of money in his wallet.

Sometimes I found myself resentful of other couples. Why were they happy and I wasn't? The feelings came when I least expected it. Romantic holidays like Valentine's Day were the worst. I didn't like to see other couples holding hands and enjoying one another talking at restaurants. Why hadn't my marriage been a happy one? How did they get so fortunate?

It is difficult to watch those we consider evil or those who have hurt us prosper. We want them to be punished and never to be blessed. If the ex gets a new car or a new item we feel he or she does not deserve, it is easy to become insulted. Prepare yourself, because eventually your ex will probably begin a dating relationship with someone. Of course it will have an effect on you, but if you find yourself angry or your behavior changes negatively towards your ex, you may have some unresolved resentment issues.

What Causes Resentment?

The number one reason why many feel resentment is when they feel like others are trying to tell them what to do or how to live their lives. This is true for me as well as I was resentful of those who made up their minds to inform me I should never have divorced. I felt an intense desire to tell them to mind their own business. Being lied about is another for me. I hate it when others lie about me or make up things about me to make themselves look better. Why was it assumed that I was a she-devil because I no longer wanted to be married to my pastor husband? Why did anyone assume that everything was my fault?

Lastly, I felt resentment when others acted superior to me. During a conversation with the ex, I found myself resentful when I thought he was trying to show his superiority. I remember a particular conversation that greatly annoyed me. When he reached an additional level of education he made several comments about how hard he had worked in order to achieve the next level. As he continued to speak I began to feel resentful. Why? I don't know. Maybe I felt like he was trying to prove that he was better than I was because he had obtained his doctorate.

Self-Resentment

Resentment against oneself may show up as remorse. I have encountered many individuals who resent themselves for the bad decisions they have made in their lives. Are you dealing with resentment for something you may have said or done? I have been asked if I resented or regretted marrying my ex-husband the second time around. Of course one may feel that because the second marriage ended in divorce, I regretted the decision to remarry. I am always one who looks for the bright side in everything so I am quick to mention that my daughter was the positive result of my decision to remarry my ex-husband.

Even after the second divorce was said and done, I did not resent the time I had stayed married. Had we not stayed married, I would never have moved to the Kansas City area and eventually met and married the love of my life. Of course I did not appreciate the many negative and horrible things that were said about me, but I won't allow the negativity of others to ruin me. Those who know me understand my decisions and the rest I really don't care about. I am the one who has to live my life and no one else can live for me. If I live the life everyone else wants me to live I will resent the very decisions I have made and end up miserable. No thank you.

Finally, don't let others define your resentment for you. What may be important to you may not be important to others. When my ex-husband built a brand new church building, someone had the nerve to ask if wished I had stayed with him because of his success as a pastor. One of my friends informed me that while visiting my ex-husband's church for a special event she overheard two women discussing me. One woman questioned the other regarding the whereabouts of the first wife and then stated, "Wherever she is, I'm sure she is sick looking at all of this." Obviously this woman believed I resented missing out on my ex-husband's success. When my friend couldn't take it anymore, she politely turned around and mentioned to the women, "What you ladies don't realize is that none of this meant anything to Janice and that she is really happy now." Thanks, Joann. I appreciate you and all others who have spoken up on my behalf.

"Our fatigue is often caused not by work, but by worry, frustration and resentment"
~ Dale Carnegie

Helpful Scriptures

As the ark of the Lord was entering the City of David, Michal daughter of Saul watched from a window. And when she saw King David leaping and dancing before the Lord, she despised him in her heart. 2 Samuel 6:16 (NIV)

When his brothers saw that their father loved him more than any of his brothers, they hated him and couldn't even talk nicely to him. Genesis 37:4 (CEB)

A peaceful mind gives life to the body, but jealousy rots the bones. Proverbs 14:30 (CEB)

Don't envy evil men but continue to reverence the Lord all the time, for surely you have a wonderful future ahead of you. There is hope for you yet! Proverbs 23:17-18 (TLB)

Then I realized that we work and do wonderful things just because we are jealous of others. This makes no more sense than chasing the wind. Ecclesiastes 4:4 (CEV)

Let everyone be sure that he is doing his very best, for then he will have the personal satisfaction of work well done and won't need to compare himself with someone else. Galatians 6:4 (TLB)

We are not to be like Cain, who belonged to Satan and killed his brother. Why did he kill him? Because Cain had been doing wrong and he knew very well that his brother's life was better than his. 1 John 3:12 (TLB)

Chapter 23
Worried about the Future

So I perceived that there was nothing better for human beings but to enjoy what they do because that's what they're allotted in life. Who, really, is able to see what will happen in the future? Ecclesiastes 3:22 (CEB)

As I thought about getting a divorce, the thoughts and concerns about our future consumed me. What was life going to be like if I stayed? What would my life be like in ten years? Would we be able to work out our differences and be a happily married couple again, or were we going to stay together and be old and bitter? Would we become one of those couples who sit across from each other at the restaurant and never talk to each other or worse yet, sleep in separate beds and never touch one another? I'm not sure if you saw the movie *Hope Springs* with Meryl Streep and Tommy Lee Jones. They were a couple that just co-existed in the same house, lived in separate bedrooms, and were afraid to touch one another.

On the other hand, I was worried about my future. Would I grow old alone, regretting the decision to divorce? Could I ever find love again? A controversial article published in 1986 by *Newsweek*, concluded women over 40 have a better chance of being killed in a terrorist attack than finding a husband. Even though the article was eventually proved to be false, an unmarried woman with no marriage prospects nearing her 40's could get real nervous with each passing birthday. I didn't have to look at the research, as I had several friends around my age who had never been married the first time. Those who were married and divorced had given up hope of ever finding someone else.

When talking with a friend who had divorced and remarried, he shared that his new marriage and relationship was good, but the complications of stepfamily life kept full happiness at bay. I too wanted happiness in my future and wondered if I could ever be happy being remarried.

The future of my children was also a concern for me. I didn't want to ruin their lives because of our choices. I wanted them to have a relationship with their father but I also wanted to be around more family. My financial future was of concern as I had not begun to think about child support and other money matters such as our ability to sell our home.

Believe it or not, I was even worried about my soon to be ex-husband. His job as the pastor of the church could be at risk, as he had only pastored there for a little over a year. If they kicked him out of the church, he wouldn't have enough money to pay child support and as a result, I wouldn't have an adequate amount to take care of my children.

Predicting the Future

It's very scary when we try to predict our own future. I wished I had a crystal ball to let me know what my life was going to be like in ten years. I may have even prayed to God to show me a glimpse of my future. I never got an answer, but I had a feeling He wanted me to trust Him and learn to depend solely on Him. Many days I found myself daydreaming about what the future held for all of us. I even spent much time journaling to write my own predictions. I found myself wondering what would happen.

Even worse than trying to predict the future, is constantly worrying about it. Philippians 4:6-7 (CEV) reads, "Don't worry about anything, but pray about everything. With thankful hearts offer up your prayers and requests to God. Then, because you belong to Christ Jesus, God will bless you with peace that no one can completely understand. And this peace will control the way you think and feel." With so many unknowns I couldn't help but worry as I'm sure I wasn't the first to face my future with trembling and fear.

When the anxiety became overwhelming, I found myself seeking the Bible for answers. Romans 8:28 became my mantra. "All things work together for good for those who love God and are called according to his purpose." I memorized that verse and wrote it down in several places as a reminder. The verse became my password on my computer so that every time I turned on my computer, I had to recite it to myself.

Worry Doesn't Help

Be careful not to worry too much about your future. After all worrying about it will not change your circumstances. In fact, our worry may lead us to do things we may later regret. Constant worrying can cause stress on our bodies and lead to physical illness. I don't have to be a doctor to know that excessive worry can interfere with your appetite, digestive system, blood pressure, sleep, and your ability to think straight. Worry ignites our fight or flight syndrome which produces hormones such as cortisol. The bad news about Cortisol is it can boost blood sugar levels and triglycerides leading to a host of health diseases such as immune disorders, digestive disorders, and hypertension. Having a degree in Biological Psychology, I have read numerous books and medical journals indicating the relationship between stress and disease.

Stress can also affect our behavior and lead to stress related behaviors such as overeating, cigarette smoking, or using alcohol and drugs. Why do they always show women in movies eating a pint of ice cream when they are upset? I found myself craving fatty foods which eventually led to irritable bowel syndrome. Worrying also affected my sleep, and I found myself suffering from a mild case of insomnia. I went to the drug store and bought St Johns Wart and melatonin to help me sleep. On desperate occasions, I took Tylenol PM or Benadryl. At first I was too vain to go to the doctor to request sleeping pills but eventually I had to get some help. In addition I read every article I could find on how to get a good night's sleep.

The fear of the unknown is a very real phenomenon and can affect our behaviors. However, our trust should be in God who knows our past as well as our future. The Bible says that worrying is a waste of our time and cannot add anything to our lives. Place your life in God's hand and allow Him to fill in the blanks for those areas you are most concerned about. Remember, He can turn a bad situation into a blessing.

Helpful Scriptures

Your future will be brighter by far than your past.
Job 8:7 (CEV)

Later the Lord spoke to Abram in a vision, "Abram, don't be afraid! I will protect you and reward you greatly."
Genesis 15:1(CEV)

Think of the bright future waiting for all the families of honest and innocent and peace-loving people.
Psalm 37:37 (CEV)

I know the plans I have in mind for you, declares the Lord; they are plans for peace, not disaster, to give you a future filled with hope. Jeremiah 29:11 (CEB)

But it is just as the Scriptures say, "What God has planned for people who love him is more than eyes have seen or ears have heard. It has never even entered our minds!" 1 Corinthians 2:9 (CEV)

I know you can do anything; no plan of yours can be opposed successfully. Job 42:2 (CEB)

Observe those who have integrity and watch those whose heart is right because the future belongs to persons of peace. Psalm 37:37 (CEB)

Chapter 24
Self-Esteem

"Although I am blameless, I have no concern for myself; I despise my own life. Job 9:21 (NIV)

Even though I was the one that wanted the divorce the second time around, my overall self-esteem suffered a blow. I began to ask questions of myself including, "What's wrong with me that I can't stay married for more than seven years? What's wrong with me where I would marry the same man twice, when it didn't work the first time?"

In divorce number one, he pushed the envelope and filed for divorce. When you are the one filed on, you may begin to doubt yourself. Again, "What's wrong with me?" is the number one question. Am I not loveable? Is there something wrong with the way I look? Am I crazy? Divorcing a minister added a whole different level of self-esteem issues. Am I not holy enough? Having been a pretty secure person most of my life, I began to doubt myself and wonder if I was the Jezebel others were making me out to be. Sometimes such comments provoked anger, while other times I wanted to crawl in a hole and disappear.

When I was angry, I wanted to lash out at the world, or gladly point out to those who were criticizing me that they were no better than I was. Yes, I could have talked about everybody else's dirty laundry and all of the messed up marriages I was aware of, but I chose to keep silent, because I knew who I was. As Madea says, "It's not what they call you it's what you answer to." Most of all I wanted to defend myself and tell the world my silence did not mean I was guilty.

Don't worry, if you had a decent self-esteem prior to the divorce, there's a good chance you will eventually get back to normal. Thank God, because I was really beginning to wonder about myself. However, if you had doubts about yourself in the first place, you may need professional help. The question has even been asked, which came first the low self-esteem or the divorce?

Remedies for Poor Self-Esteem

How can you deal with your own self-esteem issues? First you have to make peace with yourself and admit you are struggling. Admit your fears and insecurities to God because He understands and can do something about what you are experiencing. Are you angry with yourself, or have you not forgiven those who have hurt you? Find someone you can talk to. Perhaps you can speak with someone who has experienced a similar situation and survived. Other Christians can pray for you and build you up where you are torn down.

Best friends can do wonders for self-esteem because a friend can remind you of how wonderful and resilient you are and make you smile. Make new friends who enjoy doing the same things you enjoy. Join a new group with those who have similar interests or hobbies. If you feel you need professional help, call your EAP hotline and make an appointment to see a counselor. Hire a divorce coach or find a divorce prayer partner like myself. When you do have the opportunity to talk to someone, don't hold back, let it all out.

Being in the limelight, I was afraid to talk to just anyone, so I had to rely on my dear journal. In my journal I could record all my thoughts and feelings without worrying about being judged. I kept my journals in a secret place. In these days and times you can keep a journal on your smart phone and verbally record your thoughts rather than having to take the time to write everything down. Journals can be protected with a pass code. You don't have to worry about the old journals we used as a kid with the cheap lock on them leaving your private thoughts unprotected.

When your self-esteem is suffering, it is a good time to sit down and focus on some self-love. First of all forgive yourself and stop the self-blame. Divorce happens to many people for many reasons. Quit playing the old tapes in your mind and focusing on what you could have or should have done. Let the negativity go. Stop focusing on your past and start looking towards a better and brighter future.

Do something fun that you enjoy doing. Re-read your favorite encouraging book, or find a new one. Spend an afternoon at the library if you are a book lover and find two or three books you can read in your quiet time. Find some books on tape to listen to in your car. I love going to the library to find a book on a topic I am interested in. Being a lifelong learner, I love learning new things. When you find yourself wanting to have a pity party, watch a movie that will make you laugh. Learn to enjoy being by yourself. Write a love letter to yourself and include scriptures of God's love for you.

Above all take care of yourself. If you have put on a few pounds due to stress, make the decision that you are going to be physically active. Find a local fitness center or gym or yoga studio. If you don't have money to purchase a gym membership, map out a route in your neighborhood to walk at least four days a week or download an exercise routine on your computer or smart phone. If you really want a challenge, find a local marathon in your area and make up your mind to participate and finish. Resist the desire to become a couch potato. Get up and move around. Choose to live a healthier life by changing your diet. Stay away from junk foods like soda, ice cream, fried foods, or other things you crave when you are stressed. Eat more fruits and vegetables. Stay away from alcohol.

Looking better will do wonders for your self-esteem. Freshen up your wardrobe by getting rid of the things that are not flattering for you. We actually wear twenty percent of our clothes eighty percent of the time. Quit putting on the same boring outfits every week. If you are like me and wear black most of the time, infuse some bright colors into your wardrobe. If your weight has changed either way, find a seamstress or a tailor and make the necessary adjustments so that your clothes fit. Buy a couple of outfits that look fabulous on you. Wear them well and accept the compliments.

Wear accessories. Get a new hair-do, cut your hair, or color your hair. I once heard that if you go two weeks without getting a compliment on your hair, you should change something. Again, if money is an issue, go to the cosmetic counter at your local department store or call a Mary Kay beauty consultant and get a free makeover. I love getting a pedicure and will save my lunch money if I have to just to get one at least every eight weeks. When I am really stressed and my muscles tense up to the point I get headaches, I schedule a full body massage. Perhaps you are not the diva type and none of these things appeal to you.

Find out what does and do it! Men, do something for yourself that makes you feel handsome.

A Word a Day Keeps the Stress Away

Choose to spend more time with God in prayer and meditation. Set a goal to read your Bible every day. Make a commitment to read through the entire Bible in a year. Memorize encouraging scriptures. Participate in a ministry at your church where you can use your God-given gifts. If you don't know what your gifts are, take a spiritual gifts inventory online. Meet other divorced or singles at your church that can be a support and encouragement for you. Stay away from friends who want to complain. Find positive people to connect with and make sure you hang around people who build you up.

> "You must love yourself before you love another. By accepting yourself and fully being what you are, your simple presence can make others happy." - Anonymous

Helpful Scriptures

A person may think their own ways are right, but the Lord weighs the heart. Proverbs 21:2 (NIV)

I am what I am by God's grace, and God's grace hasn't been for nothing. In fact, I have worked harder than all the others—that is, it wasn't me but the grace of God that is with me. 1 Corinthians 15:10 (CEB)

Instead, we are God's accomplishment, created in Christ Jesus to do good things. God planned for these good things to be the way that we live our lives. Ephesians 2:10 (CEB)

Even the hairs on your head are all counted. Don't be afraid. You are worth more than many sparrows. Luke 12:7 (CEB)

But you are a chosen race, a royal priesthood, a holy nation, a people who are God's own possession. You have become this people so that you may speak of the wonderful acts of the one who called you out of darkness into his amazing light. 1 Peter 2:9 (CEB)

I can do all things through Christ which strengthens me. Philippians 4:13 (KJV)

And I praise you because of the wonderful way you created me. Everything you do is marvelous! Of this I have no doubt. Psalm 139:14 (CEV)

Chapter 25
Regret

He was very sorry that he had made them.
Genesis 6:6 (CEV)

REGRET: a sense of loss, disappointment, dissatisfaction, etc.; a feeling of sorrow or remorse for a fault, act, loss, disappointment, etc. (Dictionary.com).

Soon you will find yourself regretting things you may have done in your life. You may wish you had never been married in the first place. You may think about what would have happened if you never met your spouse. What if you had never let your friends convince you to go to the event where you met your spouse? What if you had gone to college somewhere else? What if? What if?

On the flip side, some of you may regret initiating or giving in to the divorce process and desire to start all over again. In some cases you can, so don't rule out reconciliation; however, in some situations the former spouse has already moved on and even remarried. Regret can happen at any time, but most often when there is some type of nostalgia involved.

When holidays come around and I can't be with my children because they have plans with their father, I regret being divorced. These feelings typically occur in relation to my children. Would they be different if we had not divorced? Would they have a better chance at having their own successful relationships if we had stayed together? As soon as the events are over my thoughts fortunately return to normal and I am okay with the decisions I have made.

We Cannot Change the Past

The past is over and we cannot go back and undo any of our actions. We may have to forgive ourselves for bad decisions and accept responsibility for our behavior. If we have harmed others in the process, it may be a good idea to seek their forgiveness. Harmful words were exchanged that cannot be taken back. Money was spent and taken that cannot be replaced. You may have lost items of personal value that were passed down through many generations in your family. Don't worry about trying to undo anything; instead, accept the fact that we cannot change our past but we can influence our future. Focus on the future and what it will take to start a new baseline and keep moving forward.

Learn Your Lesson

If you do feel like you made mistakes, don't wallow in the muck and the mire, learn from your mistakes. Maybe you said some things you shouldn't have said and did some things that were unbecoming of you and totally out of your character. Don't dwell on your mistakes; instead, focus on what you have learned in the process. For example, I was frustrated when I realized a friend I had confided in was the person spreading rumors about me. I regretted talking with the person, but couldn't undo the conversation. I learned my lesson and thought twice before opening my mouth to the wrong person.

By stopping to take a look at the past, I learned many qualities about myself. I learned what my pressure points are and my vulnerabilities. I understand the words or behaviors that provoke me to anger and avoid those situations. I learned who my friends were and who I could trust. There are so many lessons to be learned.

If you find yourself playing old tapes in your head about mistakes you have made, write them down and then write down the corresponding lesson you have learned. Write down what you would do differently if confronted with the same situation again. Prepare yourself to not repeat the same blunders again.

It Won't Happen Again

At times I regretted being so trusting and eventually made some definitive statements such as, "That will never happen to me again." On a few occasions I felt attacked and was hurt emotionally. After I cried my eyes out and washed my face, I made the decision that I wouldn't let anyone get to me in that way. In the words of Mary Mary, I told myself, "I cried my last tear yesterday." I could hear Mary J Blige singing in my ears, " I'm not gon' cry, I'm not gon' cry, I'm not gon' shed no tears." Once I made up my mind that I would not experience the same hurt again, I grew stronger day by day.

Spending time regretting the past is useless. Again, you can't change the past so quit focusing on it. You can't drive forward staring out of the rear-view mirror, but every now and then a quick glance will keep you from making the same mistakes and keep you on the right track. Your mantra should be Philippians 3:13-14 (NKJV) "Brethren, I do not count myself to have apprehended; but one thing I do, forgetting those things which are behind and reaching forward to those things which are ahead, I press toward the goal for the prize of the upward call of God in Christ Jesus."

Helpful Scriptures

He said to Moses, "Sir, please don't punish us for doing such a foolish thing." Numbers 12:11 (CEV)

And shout, "I hated advice and correction! I paid no attention to my teachers, Proverbs 5:12-13 (CEV)

Then I decided to find out all I could about wisdom and foolishness. Soon I realized that this too was as senseless as chasing the wind. The more you know, the more you hurt; the more you understand, the more you suffer. Ecclesiastes 1:17-18 (CEV)

Judas had betrayed Jesus, but when he learned that Jesus had been sentenced to death, he was sorry for what he had done. He returned the thirty silver coins to the chief priests and leaders. Matthew 27:3 (CEV)

But what good did you receive from the things you did? All you have to show for them is your shame, and they lead to death. Romans 6:21 (CEV)

My guilt has overwhelmed me like a burden too heavy to bear. Psalm 38:4 (NIV)

Finally, he came to his senses and said, "My father's workers have plenty to eat, and here I am, starving to death!" Luke 15:17 (CEV)

AFTER DIVORCE

The Catalyst for a Highly Favored Life

Chapter 26
Happy Anniversary

I think of times gone by, of those years long ago.
Psalm 77:5 (CEV)

As a married person you may have celebrated many anniversaries, including the day you met, your first date, your engagement date, and your wedding anniversary. Couples find all kinds of anniversary dates to celebrate one another. Some celebrate the day of their first kiss, or the date they were introduced to the parents, or the day they realized they were in love. People love to celebrate milestones and I was no different. I loved writing in my journal so I recorded and remembered dates for all kinds of events. When the word divorce entered our lives, I soon forgot most of our special anniversary dates and could only remember the wedding anniversary. Suddenly I had a new anniversary date to remember—the date our divorce was final.

For some reason, divorce one and two's anniversary date ended up being around a holiday. The divorce dockets are empty close to Christmas and especially on Valentine's Day. The first time around we divorced the week before Christmas, and the second time we divorced on the love day—February 14th. If we didn't take the Valentine's Day appointment, it meant waiting for another two to three weeks. I was hesitant to get a divorce on Valentine's Day, but thought why not since the day was no longer going to be the same anyway. I thought to myself, "I just want to get this over with."

After divorce two, I remember sitting in Bible study on a Wednesday night when I glanced at the calendar and suddenly realized the day was my former wedding anniversary date. I don't know how I missed the date, after all I did go to work earlier in the day and glanced at the calendar several times. Immediately I felt like a ton of bricks had fallen on me and my eyes hit a water gusher. I put my bible down, dashed out of the sanctuary, and headed to the ladies room to cry in peace. As soon as I closed the door, I cried and wailed like a baby. It felt good to get it all out.

Then I was faced with a dilemma. How was I going to get my stuff and go home without exposing myself? When I cry, I look like all hell has broken loose. My face is beet red and my eyes are swollen and bloodshot. I suffer from dry eye disease which makes it difficult for me to make tears. A crying episode for me requires more than a box of Kleenex, it requires a cold, wet compress placed over my eyes overnight for the swelling to go down. All I had in the bathroom were toilet paper and paper towels.

After crying my eyes out, I really needed to get out of the church and home to my own bed. There was no way I was going to get out of there without someone noticing I had been crying. Just as I was praying and contemplating how to get out of the bathroom undetected, I heard a faint knock at the door. The Lord had sent someone to help me. I opened the door and found a fellow church member by the name of Michelle who was part of the singles' ministry. Michelle asked, "Are you okay?"

I tried to mumble "yes" but one look at me and she could tell I was not okay. Trying to pull myself together, I asked her to gather my things out of the Bible study class so I could make a quick exit. Once she retrieved my things, I thanked her and asked her to pray for me as I had just realized it was my former anniversary and the date had caught me off guard. I don't know why I was so bothered by realizing what day it was. After all, almost an entire year had gone by.

Divorce Party

A couple of years ago one of my coworkers was going through a divorce and sent out invitations for her "divorce party." I had no idea there was such a thing and didn't know what to make of it so I did not attend. According to those who attended, the party included a ceremony where the guest of honor jumped backwards over the broom to signify the end of the marriage. Those who attended said the party was a blast!

Did you know there are divorce party planners out there who get paid to help people plan divorce parties? There is a woman by the name of Christine Gallagher who is the author of *The Divorce Party Planner: How to Throw a Divorce or Breakup Party.* I glanced at the website divorceplanner.com where you can find everything imaginable for a successful event. Evidently having a divorce party helps you to cope with your transition. According to the website a divorce party is an opportunity to vent, cry, laugh, yell, or do whatever you need to do in the company of loving friends and family. They say it's the perfect way to announce your new status as a single person. Hmmm. Not sure I would have ever thrown a party, but if it suits you, go for it. Then maybe you will have two new anniversary dates; the date of your divorce and the date of your official divorce party.

Helpful Scriptures

Human one, write down today's date, because today the king of Babylon has set up camp at Jerusalem—today!
Ezekiel 24:2 (CEB)

So take it to heart from this day forward, from the twenty-fourth day of the ninth month. Take it to heart from the day when the foundation for the LORD's temple was laid.
Haggai 2:18 (CEB)

Don't ask, "How is it that the former days were better than these?" Because it isn't wise to ask this.
Ecclesiastes 7:10 (CEB)

Oh, for the days when I was in my prime, when God's intimate friendship blessed my house, when the Almighty was still with me and my children were around me, when my path was drenched with cream and the rock poured out for me streams of olive oil. Job 29:4-6 (NIV)

I think it's right that I keep stirring up your memory, as long as I'm alive. 2 Peter 1:13 (CEB)

Look! I'm creating a new heaven and a new earth: past events won't be remembered; they won't come to mind.
Isaiah 65:17 (CEB)

Good people are remembered long after they are gone, but the wicked are soon forgotten. Proverbs 10:7 (CEV)

Chapter 27
Embarrassed to Say "I'm Divorced"

And he fixed his gaze and stared at him, until he was embarrassed. And the man of God wept.
2 Kings 8:11 (ESV)

I remember the first time I had to complete a survey that gave the option of the following boxes:
☐ Single
☐ Married
☐ Divorced

Even though I completed forms like this a million times on paper and online, the first time I had to check the divorced box I felt devastated. Not wanting to lie on the form, I attempted to skip the question, but an answer was required. Somehow, I didn't want complete strangers to know that I was now in the divorced category. If you think checking a box was difficult, try saying, "I'm divorced" aloud for the first time, second time, and even for a few years.

One of the most difficult experiences for me was moving to a different church with my children in tow and having to get acclimated to a new fellowship. I didn't want them to think that I was a single mom, but didn't like the idea of having to admit that I was divorced. I guess I was worried about people judging me.

Why is it embarrassing to admit being divorced? Is there the fear of others being judgmental? Is there the fear of our testimony being ruined? It's almost easier to say I'm separated because divorce is such a negative word. I told a friend the title I had selected for this book and tears began to form in her eyes. I was concerned about her response and asked her if I had said something wrong. She shared with me that she still feels stigmatized by having to admit she failed at marriage not only once, but twice. Even though her last divorce was more than five years ago, the pain and embarrassment was still there.

Can You Say Divorced?

My current husband indicates it was five years before he felt comfortable saying the word divorce. He avoided having conversations in which his divorce was the topic. He didn't mention the word and absolutely never preached a sermon about divorce. His preferred statement was, "We are not together right now." Even after we were married he found it difficult to admit being divorced. Instead he said, "I'm remarried."

The Bible offers a remedy for our emotional shame when admitting being divorced. Read John 4:1-42 where Jesus meets the Samaritan woman at the well. This woman needed water for her household but deliberately came to the well at midday as to avoid others. Having been divorced five times, she was probably the subject of much gossip in her town. Jesus knew she had been married five times and took the time to minister to her to let her know she was worthy of salvation. After her conversation with Jesus, she was no longer ashamed and ran throughout the community to tell others Jesus told her everything about her past. In fact, she set the record for being the catalyst for a whole town getting saved.

After encountering Jesus, she wasn't worried about the gossip and what other's thought of her. This story did wonders for me. I hope it will encourage you as well. Just because you are divorced, it does not mean that God no longer loves you or that He is mad at you. In fact He wants to go out of his way as he did for the woman at the well to redeem you. Now, I can not only admit that I am divorced, but tell the world, "I am Divorced and Still Highly Favored."

Do you hide from other people or neglect to tell them about your divorce because of embarrassment? Children of divorced parents also have difficulty talking about their parent's marital status following a divorce. Some say, "My parents don't live in the same house." If you overhear your child avoiding the issue, don't become angry or take it personally. Children need time to adjust and may be two years behind their parents in getting used to the change.

The good news is over time it gets easier to check boxes and to admit your divorce status. Remarriage helps but it is not required. Practice saying to yourself, "I'm divorced." Try this statement: "I was married but now I'm divorced" or "I was married for 10 years and then we divorced." Sooner or later you will find yourself no longer embarrassed but glad you are able to say it without wondering what the other person thinks. The best part is when you realize that others may not really care about your marital status.

Helpful Scriptures

Elisha stared at him until Hazael was embarrassed, then Elisha began crying. 2 Kings 8:11 (CEV)

Then Memucan told the king and the officials: Your Majesty, Queen Vashti has not only embarrassed you, but she has insulted your officials and everyone else in all the provinces. Esther 1:16 (CEV)

I am embarrassed every day, and I blush with shame. Psalm 44:15 (CEV)

Maybe I brag a little too much about the authority that the Lord gave me to help you and not to hurt you. Yet I am not embarrassed to brag. 2 Corinthians 10:8 (CEV)

So I confessed my sins and told them all to you. I said, "I'll tell the LORD each one of my sins." Then you forgave me and took away my guilt. Psalm 32:5 (CEV)

Jesus told her, "Go and bring your husband" The woman answered, "I don't have a husband." "That's right," Jesus replied, "you're telling the truth. You don't have a husband. You have already been married five times, and the man you are now living with isn't your husband." The woman said, "Sir, I can see that you are a prophet. John 4:16-19 (CEV)

You were like a young wife, brokenhearted and crying because her husband had divorced her. But the LORD your God says, "I am taking you back! Isaiah 54:6 (CEV)

Chapter 28
Is It Okay For Me To Be Happy?

Make my heart glad! I serve you, and my prayer is sincere. You willingly forgive, and your love is always there for those who pray to you. Psalms 86:4-5 (CEV)

One morning, even in the midst of my turmoil, I woke up extremely happy. I wasn't sure what caused my sudden ray of sunshine, but I loved feeling that way. Nothing in my life was different. I didn't win the Publisher's Clearinghouse Sweepstakes or get a call from anyone sharing exceptionally good news; I just woke up happy. After that day, there were other pockets of happiness. It was good to feel like my old self again. I wanted to have more joyful days so I made it my personal mission to be happy. In trying to maintain my happiness I began to think of all the things I should have been thankful for.

> I had peace and quiet in my home.
> I wasn't arguing with my spouse anymore.
> God still loved me.
> I found a new church home.
> I was thankful for grace and mercy, of which I did not deserve.
> My children seemed like they were doing okay.
> My children liked their new schools.

Just because you are going through or gone through a divorce does not mean that you have to walk around sad and angry all the time. My prayer for you is that over time you will experience both joy and happiness. As the song writer says, "This joy I have, the world didn't give it to me. The world didn't give it and the world can't take it away." I was thankful for those pockets of joy that came and sometimes went. I had a joy knowing that despite what was going on in my life, God was there for me. I was happy for his forgiveness and grace and mercy. I was happy I could still praise him in the middle of turmoil.

Make a decision to wake up happy in the morning. Spend some time in the word meditating on scriptures about God's goodness. Make people wonder what in the world you are so happy about. There is nothing wrong with being happy even in the midst of one of the most difficult times in your life. Give them something to talk about.

Laughter is Great Medicine

Start laughing again. They say laughter is good for the soul. Even the Bible says in Proverbs 17:22, "A cheerful heart is good medicine." Humor is a powerful and effective way to heal resentments, disagreements, and hurts. In my reading, I discovered that laughter declines dramatically as people age. That means, the older we get the more creative we need to be to keep laughing. Studies show that children on average laugh 400 times a day, compared to adults who laugh only 17 times a day. Laughter expert and psychology professor, Dr. Rod Martin at Western University in Ontario, Canada, recommends laughing at least 100 times a day.

Do you have some catching up to do? Try some of these suggestions to infuse laughter in your day. Call a friend who makes you laugh. Watch a television show that will have you in stitches. Download or rent a comedy movie. Go on the internet and subscribe to the joke of the day. Have you been to Wilma Jones' internet site for divorced women? Visit her community at Livinghappierafter.com.

A great way to move towards laughing is by first smiling. It's the beginning of laughter. Bring humor into your conversations—share funny thoughts throughout the day with those you interact with. Do something silly. Stop taking yourself so seriously and make the commitment to laugh more. Start today!

Helpful Scriptures

What happiness for those whose guilt has been forgiven! What joys when sins are covered over! What relief for those who have confessed their sins and God has cleared their record. Psalms 32:1-2 (TLB)

Look, happy is the person whom God corrects; so don't reject the Almighty's instruction. Job 5:17 (CEB)

Taste and see how good the LORD is! The one who takes refuge in him is truly happy! Psalm 34:8 (CEB)

Those who put their trust in the LORD, who pay no attention to the proud or to those who follow lies, are truly happy! Psalm 40:4 (CEB)

Those who live in your house are truly happy; they praise you constantly. Selah. Psalm 84:4 (CEB)

Shout triumphantly to the LORD, all the earth! Be happy! Rejoice out loud! Sing your praises! Psalm 98:4 (CEB)

Happy are those who strive for peace—they shall be called the sons of God. Matthew 5:9 (TLB)

If any of you are suffering, they should pray. If any of you are happy, they should sing. James 5:13 (CEB)

Chapter 29
Gratitude

All these things are for your benefit. As grace increases to benefit more and more people, it will cause gratitude to increase, which results in God's glory.
2 Corinthians 4:15 (CEB)

While going through a divorce you may tend to think about all of the problems and heartache and forget to be grateful. There were times I was angry with the world, but mostly at my ex because in my mind everything was his fault. I found myself complaining more. I wasn't happy with my job, my wardrobe, my car, or anything I could find to criticize. I didn't grumble or whine to others mainly because I hated when others grumbled openly to me about their circumstances.

It was not my personality to be unhappy, so I was determined to improve my moods and attitude. In my reading, I discovered a gratitude journal was a great way to keep yourself thankful and in a positive state of mind. I had plenty of new journals around the house, so I picked out a lovely pink one to start recording grateful thoughts.

A Gratitude Journal

At the top of every page of my journal I wrote the date and the following statement: Today, I am grateful for _____. My list seemed silly at first as I listed people, places, and things. I was grateful for my children, my parents, and my friends. I was grateful for having a job, a closet full of clothes, a house I could afford, and a neighborhood with a lot of other kids for my children to play with. I was pleased my children were doing well in school. I was thankful I was receiving child support on time every month. I was glad I had sisters and my mom to have heart-to-heart conversations with. Having enough money to buy Christmas gifts was comforting. I was really thankful to have a townhouse with a garage, so I didn't have to scrape my windows off in the winter. Meeting new friends at church was refreshing. The list goes on and on. As I dedicated myself to writing down what I was grateful for I began to feel somewhat better about my life despite my predicament.

GRATITUDE TO GOD

The more I began to show gratitude for what was going well in my life, the better life seemed. However, writing a gratitude list was not sufficient to make the real changes I desired in my life. My gratitude seemed dependent on finding enough items to write to convince myself that life wasn't so bad after all. I was starting to run out of things to write, or found myself writing the same list over and over. Soon I began to write what I wished to happen in my life that I could be thankful for. Soon my gratitude journal turned into a wish list. I was using my gratitude journal based on Proverbs 23:7, "*As a man thinketh, so is he.*" I was going to speak good things into my life and thank God for each and every blessing.

You have to be careful with gratitude journals because you can easily give yourself credit for the positive things that happen in your life. The real reason I even had things to be grateful for in the first place was because of God's grace and mercy. His grace and mercy was the reason I was not destroyed, but I was not showing my gratitude to Him. My prayer life at this point was pretty much having a list of things I needed God to do for me during my life transition. My prayer journal contained daily requirements I needed from God including emergency requests.

I know it's hard, but start a gratitude journal and write down all the things you are grateful for even while you are going through this difficult time. I remember a hymn that says, "Count your blessings, name them one by one. Count your blessings see what God has done." Be grateful for the supportive friends who have stood by your side during this difficult time. Be thankful even for the old friends who have shown their true colors and who have abandoned you. Be grateful for the loving kindness and forgiveness God has extended towards you.

Instead of thinking about what you have lost, it's a good idea to be grateful for what you do have. Perhaps you are blessed with children. If you hadn't married in the first place you would never have your unique children. Even though both of my children look more like their father than they look like me, I was grateful he had fathered my children. The entire marriage was not horrible, there were some good memories. Cherish the happy moments in your marriage and don't dwell on what led to the divorce. Make a photo album for your children and include pictures from when your marriage was happy.

Gratitude Has Benefits

There are other benefits for focusing on what is going well in your life. Gratitude can help you feel better about your life overall giving you optimism about the future. Those who show gratitude have fewer health problems. Gratitude can also improve your sleep. In the article "Counting Your Blessings: How Gratitude Improves your Health," there are five suggestions: 1) keep a daily gratitude journal; 2) use visual reminders, such as post it notes; 3) find a gratitude partner; 4) make a public commitment to be grateful; or 5) change your self-talk.

A friend of mine exposed me to Will Bowen's complaint free world (www.willbowen.com). Followers wear a purple bracelet to remind them not to complain. It comes with a complete set of rules on what to do when we want to complain and other helpful tips to help refocus our thoughts on anything but complaining.

The late Maya Angelou has a famous quote: "If you don't like something, change it. If you can't change it, change your attitude. Don't complain." I agree with her. We have the ability to do something about the things we complain about. If circumstances are beyond our control, we can stay frustrated or move on to the areas we can control. By now you know that you cannot change your ex; however, you can change you attitude. Don't use up all of your energy complaining about the ex. Use your energy being thankful you are moving on. Remember, gratitude can be expressed in many ways—through prayer, writing a gratitude list daily, and through meditation. Whatever method you use, make the decision to add some gratitude to your day and watch the world become a better place. You will soon begin to realize that even though you are divorced, you are still highly favored!

Helpful Scriptures

The word of Christ must live in you richly. Teach and warn each other with all wisdom by singing psalms, hymns, and spiritual songs. Sing to God with gratitude in your hearts. Colossians 3:16 (CEB)

Therefore, since we are receiving a kingdom that can't be shaken, let's continue to express our gratitude. With this gratitude, let's serve in a way that is pleasing to God with respect and awe, because our God really is a consuming fire. Hebrews 12:28-29 (CEB)

When I asked for your help, you answered my prayer and gave me courage. Psalm 138:3 (CEV)

I'm grateful to God, whom I serve with a good conscience as my ancestors did. I constantly remember you in my prayers day and night. 2 Timothy 1:3 (CEB)

Give thanks in every situation because this is God's will for you in Christ Jesus. 1 Thessalonians 5:18 (CEB)

Each one of you is part of the body of Christ, and you were chosen to live together in peace. So let the peace that comes from Christ control your thoughts. And be grateful. Colossians 3:15 (CEV)

Every time I think of you, I thank my God. Philippians 1:3 (CEV)

Praise the LORD and pray in his name! Tell everyone what he has done. 1 Chronicles 16:8 (CEV)

CHAPTER 30
Self-Reflection

Search me, God, and know my heart; test me and know my anxious thoughts. See if there is any offensive way in me, and lead me in the way everlasting.
Psalms 139:23-24 (NIV)

As I was going through the divorce process, the thought that constantly lingered in the corner of my mind was, "Is there something wrong with me? Or did I do something that destined me to fail at marriage?" Throughout the process, I chose to focus much of the blame on my ex rather than focus on myself. It was much easier to believe the breakdown in our marriage was his fault. No need to think about myself. After all I was a perfect wife and mother, right?

Once my life began to settle down and I was living the new normal, I had a great deal of time to think. In my alone time, I pondered my life experiences and what the future might hold for me. Would I ever consider dating again? What did I want out of life and relationships? Did I ever want to marry again? What did I have to offer someone else? What were my beliefs about life and love? What had I learned from my marriage and divorce experiences? Was I the Godly woman that I proclaimed to be? If someone asked me what I would do differently next time, what would I say? I thought about myself, what others may think of me, and what others were saying about me. So many questions went through my head. I tried to journal so I could later reflect on my thought processes.

We all make mistakes in life, but it is important that our errors are not made in vain. I definitely made numerous mistakes beginning with my first marriage. There were problems in the first marriage that were still not resolved in our second marriage. Why did we get remarried in the first place? Was I influenced by others? Was I fooling myself thinking both of us had changed? Was I believing the myth that absence makes the heart grow fonder? Or was I trying to prove something to those who criticized me and looked at me with dismay every Sunday morning? The second marriage was not a mistake because during the seven year period, our daughter was born. She was the blessing from our re-marriage.

How to Self-Reflect

In order to learn from your mistakes you have to dissect your experiences and take a good hard look at yourself. I was overdue for some self-reflection and insight into my thought processes and behaviors. Here are some suggestions to help you get started on the road of self-reflection and insight.

Your Thoughts and Beliefs – What are the tapes playing over and over in your head? How do you view others? Are you trying to control your own life or are you being guided by the Holy Spirit? Are you able to trust others? Do you see the glass as half empty or half full? Are you willing to trust God with your future, or are you going to try to control it again yourself? Do you understand what marriage is really about and what unconditional love means?

Your View of Love – What is your view of the opposite sex? What did you learn about love and relationships growing up in your home? Watching my parents' relationship taught me that I wanted marriage for everything else but love. I don't remember seeing my parents in their happy years and can't remember seeing them loving up on each other. I can't remember seeing them laughing a whole lot or enjoying one another. I can only remember a couple of times as a young child when they got dressed up and went out on a date together. My mom was very involved in the church and raising us and my dad contributed to the home financially not emotionally. My lack of relationship with my own father gave me the belief that if I have my own money, I really didn't need to depend on a man to take care of me.

VICTIM OR VICTOR?

Are you a victim or a victor? Do you believe that you are permanently damaged goods because you are divorced? Do you believe you are a victim and have no control over what happens in your life? If you have a victim mentality, life can be depressing, thinking everyone is out to get you. Choose to be a victor, believing you have choices and knowing, you can do all things through Christ who strengthens you" (Philippians 4:13).

YOUR WORDS

What kind of words do you use in the course of a day? Are you complaining about what you don't have? Are you criticizing others and gossiping? Are you using kind words when talking with others? Are you talking about things that matter or babbling just to hear yourself? Are you engaging in a friendly manner with others? How are you communicating in written words such as texts and emails? Are you offering encouragement to others? Are you constantly bringing up the past and talking about your misery? After listening to others, I had to make a conscious choice to have positive thoughts and speak positive words.

YOUR BEHAVIOR – What do you need to do differently? What do you need to change? What are you doing that you need to stop doing? What do you need to do more of? What are you doing right? Maybe you need to stop going by the donut shop every morning for a pastry which isn't healthy for you. Maybe you need to spend more time around positive people or join a support group or make new friends. Maybe you can change your spending habits.

YOUR FAITH – Where are you in your faith journey? Do you trust that God will provide for you regardless of your circumstances? Do you believe that God still loves you even though you are divorced? Do you believe that God is mad at you? Do you trust that God has your best interest at heart? Once everything is all said and done and your life is beginning to settle down to the new normal, it is time to take a look in the mirror and do some self-reflection. Stopping to take a look at one's self means looking at ourselves through God's eyes rather than our own.

Consider this quote on self-reflection:

> "The true purpose of self-reflection is to correct our mistaken thoughts and actions and learn from them, thereby creating a more constructive life. Self-reflection is not just the simple act of discovering past mistakes and making up for these mistakes, like resetting a negative to zero. The ultimate objective of self-reflection is the development of a more positive self and the realization of a utopia on earth as the fulfilment of God's will" (Okawa 2008).

Helpful Scriptures

Examine yourselves to see whether you are in the faith; test yourselves. Do you not realize that Christ Jesus is in you—unless, of course, you fail the test? And I trust that you will discover that we have not failed the test. Now we pray to God that you will not do anything wrong—not so that people will see that we have stood the test but so that you will do what is right even though we may seem to have failed. 2 Corinthians 13:5-7 (NIV)

How many wrongs and sins have I committed? Show me my offense and my sin. Job 13:23 (NIV)

Test me, Lord, and try me, examine my heart and my mind. Psalm 26:2 (NIV)

We must search and examine our ways; we must return to the Lord. Lamentations 3:40 (CEB)

I thought about the wrong direction in which I was headed, and turned around and came running back to you. Psalm 119:59 (TLB)

But if we had judged ourselves, we wouldn't be judged. 1 Corinthians 11:31 (CEB)

Now this is what the Lord Almighty says: "Give careful thought to your ways. Haggai 1:5 (NIV)

Chapter 31
Lead Us Not Into Temptation

You are tempted in the same way that everyone else is tempted. But God can be trusted not to let you be tempted too much, and he will show you how to escape from your temptations. 1 Corinthians 10:13 (CEV)

Why is it that the things we say we will never do, we end up doing them? The apostle Paul had the same problem when he wrote Romans 7:21 "It seems to be a fact of life that when I want to do what is right, I inevitably do what is wrong." (TLB) Most of you probably made the statement, "I will never get divorced." I made the statement twice, and had to eat my words each time. Sad but true, if you are reading this book you may remember saying something similar.

The truth is, saying what we won't do sets us up for temptation. What is temptation? Dictionary.com defines tempt: *the fact or state of being tempted, especially to evil or temptation; is being enticed or allured to do something often regarded as unwise, wrong, or immoral.* Divorce is full of temptation. Enticements are present in every place, condition, and relationship. First we may be tempted to go places we typically would not go. After my divorce was final, my girlfriends wanted to get me out of the house, so they invited me to go out to a club on Friday and Saturday nights. The club is fine if that is what you like to do, but a former first lady would definitely get talked about if she showed up in the club. So clubbing wasn't an option for me.

I had very good friends who happened to be males, but it was not a good idea to be out hanging with any of them or visiting them at their homes or inviting them to my home. Other temptations included wanting to stay in the bed on Sunday mornings and not face the crowd at church.

Divorce is tough, especially financially. Shopping was one of my favorite past times and I enjoyed finding great deals. Being stressed, I was tempted to go out and spend a lot of money to make me feel better. Spending money really was attractive when the divorce wasn't final and I knew my ex would have to be responsible for paying the credit card bills. On the other hand, money was tight and I considered going out to find a part-time job. The job would bring in additional income, but I would rob my children of precious time that they needed with me. I even thought about exaggerating my financial needs to make my ex pay through the nose.

Relationship Temptations

Relationship temptations are the toughest during the divorce process. First of all, the relationship between you and your future ex is at its worst. You want to say and do some outlandish things. You may have imagined yourself inflicting personal body harm or had visions of something harmful happening to him or her. Be careful, your imagination can plant outrageously cruel thoughts in your mind. You may be tempted to call your ex and start an argument just because you miss interacting with him or her. You may want to bad mouth your ex to your children or others who will listen. There were times I was so frustrated, I wanted to call his church members and tell them the real deal about their pastor. Doing such an outrageous act would have immediately caused more problems for me if he lost his job.

When we have been harmed emotionally we tend to want revenge. Many individuals whose spouse has cheated on them have made the mistake of retaliating by finding someone of their own to become romantically involved with. Any new romantic relationship within two years during and after the divorce can be a temptation. Your emotions are everywhere, so it is not a good time to get involved in an emotional or sexual relationship. Don't let loneliness get the best of you. Don't allow Satan to convince you a new "friend" is just what the doctor ordered. Jumping into another relationship too soon can cause you to do some things you may regret later.

Give yourself some time. But remember, Satan knows your number and may send you the most handsome, "perfect" man or the most beautiful woman in the world to get you off track. For a while, I had guys coming out of the woodwork, including reconnecting with old boyfriends. I wanted to believe it was divine intervention that they were calling me, but soon realized it was a distraction. Satan even sent an *Ebony* Magazine bachelor my way. I lost a bet with a girlfriend and as a result I had to contact one of the guys featured in the magazine's bachelor edition. Thinking I wouldn't stand a chance, I called directory assistance and got the telephone number of the bachelor that looked my age. Thankfully, I didn't get an answer so I left a message on his machine informing him I had lost a bet and had to call him. I left my contact information and informed my friend I had held up my part of the bargain by making the call.

As luck would have it, the guy was tickled by my message and was traveling in the area on business and wanted to connect with me. When he called, I was in the middle of taking a Sunday afternoon nap and mistook him for my nephew and told him I didn't have time to talk to him. He really thought I was funny and was even more intrigued by my personality. After I realized who I was talking to and tried to apologize he laughed heartily. Our conversation was uphill from there. I learned that he was a Christian, athletic, gainfully employed, fun to talk to, and had a great sense of humor. All those attributes I found attractive in a man. I wasn't worried about talking to a psycho because I was aware of the extensive background checks and psychological evaluations required for guys or ladies included in the magazine as a bachelor or bachelorette.

He ended up coming for a visit and we had a wonderful dinner date. He was a perfect gentleman. I began to think he could be my next husband sent from heaven. As he was in town for several days, he called and mentioned what a great time we had at dinner and that he wanted to spend more private time with me and invited me to his hotel room. I came to my senses and realized he had more on his mind. As tempted as I was to go, I didn't. However, I was glad he autographed my *Ebony* on our first date since I never heard from him again.

Some of you may have already gotten into relationships now that your divorce is over. Put the brakes on and take your time. There is no need to rush into another relationship. If he or she is the right one, they will wait for you. On the other hand, some of you after several years may be afraid of committing to another relationship because you don't want to get hurt again. You may make the mistake of dating and cohabitating or shacking up because you are afraid of marriage but still want companionship. Don't do it. A very strong predictor of a failed marriage is living together before marriage.

God Understands our Temptation

When we enter into temptation remember God is faithful and we can find strength and security in Him. Don't rely on your own strength, because we often fail ourselves by doing the very thing we said we wouldn't do. God knows what we can and cannot handle and will give us what we need to overcome it if we rely on Him. The extra good news according to 1 Corinthians 10:13 is that when we are tempted, God will provide a way of escape. I remember a time when I wanted to bad mouth my ex-husband. I walked towards the telephone to make a phone call when suddenly another call came in. Other times I was tempted to go somewhere in my car that I had no business going and couldn't find my keys or my car wouldn't start. God saved me on many occasions from self-destruction.

The good news is that Jesus understands temptation. Christ himself was tempted not only to teach us that it is not a sin to be tempted, but to show us what to do when we are tempted. Be prepared for temptation by being prayed up and studied up. Learn to recognize temptation for what it is—a plot to destroy you. The devil seeks to steal, kill, and destroy you, but remember God wants you to live life to the fullest. Maintain preparedness and when you see the devil getting busy, tell him to "get behind you." The Bible states if we resist the devil, he will flee from us. (James 4:7)

Helpful Scriptures

Brothers and sisters, if a person is caught doing something wrong, you who are spiritual should restore someone like this with a spirit of gentleness. Watch out for yourselves so you won't be tempted too. Galatians 6:1 (CEB)

For since he himself has now been through suffering and temptation, he knows what it is like when we suffer and are tempted, and he is wonderfully able to help us.
Hebrews 2:18 (TLB)

Don't blame God when you are tempted! God cannot be tempted by evil, and he doesn't use evil to tempt others. We are tempted by our own desires that drag us off and trap us. James 1:13-14 (CEV)

Stay alert and pray so that you won't give in to temptation. The spirit is eager, but the flesh is weak.
Matthew 26:41 (CEB)

When the devil had finished all this tempting, he left him until an opportune time. Luke 4:13 (NIV)

"Why are you sleeping?" he asked them. "Get up and pray so that you will not fall into temptation." Luke 22:46 (NIV)

It seems to be a fact of life that when I want to do what is right, I inevitably do what is wrong. Romans 7:21 (TLB)

Chapter 32
Forgiveness

But Jesus told the woman, "Because of your faith, you are now saved. May God give you peace!" Luke 7:50 (CEV)

Does getting a divorced mean that God is mad at you? Will God forgive you? Can you still live a blessed and highly favored life? Will others forgive you? Will you forgive your ex-spouse? Will your children forgive you? Will you forgive others for the terrible things said about you and to you? Can you forgive yourself? Once the divorce process is done and over, there is a lot of forgiving that must take place. Every book I write has a chapter on forgiveness because it is so important in all areas of your life.

Godly Forgiveness

In I John 1:9 the scripture states, "If we confess our sins, He is faithful and just to forgive us and cleanse us from all unrighteousness." Believe it or not, God is the last one we need to worry about when it comes to forgiveness. Why? Because God is love. He created us knowing that we would sin and yet He created us anyway. God's love is unconditional. He loves us married, single, or divorced. There is nowhere we can go to escape his endless love. Is God mad at you? Heavens no! He may be disappointed in our behavior but God always loves us unconditionally. If God can love the murderer, the thief, and others who have committed heinous crimes, he can love the divorcee.

As I stated earlier, read Joyce Meyer's book *God is Not Mad at You*. She does a wonderful job of explaining the love and forgiveness God has for us. Her book did wonders for me in accepting God's love for me regardless of my situation of status. I recommended the book to a client of mine who was dealing with the fear of God being angry at her because of her divorce. Her husband was the one who decided he wanted to divorce her because of her health and because he wanted to be with another woman. She was afraid she had failed as a wife and that God was not going to forgive her for letting him out of the marriage.

Listen up my friends, God loves you and there is nothing you can do about it so accept the love and the forgiveness He offers. If you have sinned, confess your sins and make the commitment to do better. Don't walk around with unconfessed sin. Let's learn from David's example in the Bible. As long as he tried to hide his sin which included lying, committing adultery, and even murder, God could not bless him. Even though he got caught, once he confessed his sins to God and repented of them he became the apple of God's eye. If David was forgiven and labeled a man after God's heart, surely we can do the same. If you have any unconfessed sin, do yourself a favor and spend some time conversing with God to get it all out. After all we are not hiding anything from him that he doesn't already know. He is just waiting on you so that He may grant you grace (unmerited favor) and forgiveness.

Self-Forgiveness

We all make mistakes. The key is whether or not we learn from our mistakes. If you get too close to the fire you will most likely get burned. When I was a young girl the house we lived in was heated by gas heaters in most of the rooms. Mom turned the burners off at night so we would not get carbon monoxide poisoning while we slept. We kept warm under blankets and quilts. Early in the morning before we got up, she would come back in and light the gas heaters so our rooms would be warm enough. On really cold mornings, the first thing we would do is jump out of the bed and stand in front of the heater to warm up. Mom told us if we did that to make sure we lifted up our gown so that it would not catch on fire. I forgot one morning and burnt my nightgown on the gas heater in the bathroom. The gown was extremely hot on my legs and almost burned me. Guess what? I never had that problem again, because I learned from the mistake the first time around.

Because I could not get a new nightgown until Christmas I was mad at myself for what I had done. Every night and morning I reminded myself of how stupid I was to get too close to the heater. Instead of forgiving myself, I kept beating up on myself.

As humans we will continue to make mistakes and must learn to forgive ourselves. I have made far greater mistakes than getting too close to the fire and I have had to learn to forgive myself. The Bible really doesn't talk much about self-forgiveness but the scriptures do speak to God forgiving us and remembering our sins no more. (Jeremiah 31:34.) If God is the one we have really sinned against and He doesn't bring our sins up in our face, why can't we forgive ourselves? Sure you won't be able to forget everything, but mistakes should no longer affect you in a negative way if you have forgiven yourself. Stop playing old tapes in your head that are holding you hostage. If this area is a problem for you, seek God's help. Read and study scriptures on forgiveness and learn to see yourself as forgivable.

Forgiving Others

Possibly the most difficult forgiveness for you to achieve may be forgiving others, primarily your ex. Perhaps your ex did something to violate the marriage which ultimately led to your divorce. Perhaps during the divorce process, tempers were flared and you and your ex-spouse said some very harmful words to one another. Perhaps your ex-spouse ran off with all of the money leaving you in a financial dilemma. Trust me there are many offenses that can occur during the divorce season that we may find difficult to forgive.

Can you forgive your ex? You may be saying to yourself, "I can't let him off the hook that easily for what he did to me." Forgiveness is not about letting someone off the hook. It's about freeing yourself from carrying the negative burden around regarding someone else. Many books have been written about forgiveness. If you are struggling in this area, please find a biblical book on forgiveness and read it. My favorite is *The Forgiveness Project* by Michael Barry. This book was a life changer for me. Another outstanding book is *The Book of Forgiving* by Desmond Tutu and his daughter, Mpho Tutu. I encourage you to read their book and commit to following their forgiveness process.

The four step process as outlined in the book include: 1) Telling the story; 2) Naming the hurt; 3) Granting forgiveness; and 4) Renewing or releasing the relationship. According to the Tutu's, "Without forgiveness, we remain tethered to the person who harmed us... Until we can forgive the person who harmed us, they will hold the keys to our happiness, they will be our jailor" (Tutu, 2014).

Every book on forgiveness I have read states that when we forgive others we are freeing ourselves. Holding eternal grudges and unforgiveness is like picking up hot coals and throwing them at others. You will end up burning yourself and causing self-damage, and you will most likely miss them because of the self-inflicted pain. Do yourself a favor today and forgive others for what they have done to you. Forgiveness doesn't happen overnight, but it can happen. Do it. You will thank yourself in the long run.

Helpful Scriptures

Have mercy on me, God, according to your faithful love! Wipe away my wrongdoings according to your great compassion! Wash me completely clean of my guilt; purify me from my sin! Because I know my wrongdoings, my sin is always right in front of me. Psalms 51:1-3 (CEB)

This is why I tell you that her many sins have been forgiven; so she has shown great love. The one who is forgiven little loves little." Then Jesus said to her, "Your sins are forgiven." Luke 7:47-50 (CEB)

I cry out to you from the depths, LORD— my Lord, listen to my voice! Let your ears pay close attention to my request for mercy! If you kept track of sins, LORD—my Lord, who would stand a chance? But forgiveness is with you— that's why you are honored. Psalms 130:1-4 (CEB)

"Blessed are those whose transgressions are forgiven, whose sins are covered. Blessed is the one whose sin the Lord will never count against them." Romans 4:7-8 (NIV)

Prayer that comes from faith will heal the sick, for the Lord will restore them to health. And if they have sinned, they will be forgiven. For this reason, confess your sins to each other and pray for each other so that you may be healed. The prayer of the righteous person is powerful in what it can achieve. James 5:15-16 (CEB)

Be tolerant with each other and, if someone has a complaint against anyone, forgive each other. As the Lord forgave you, so also forgive each other. Colossians 3:13 (CEB)

Chapter 33
Don't Stop Praying

Lord in the morning you hear my voice. In the morning I lay it all out before you. Then I wait expectantly.
Psalm 5:3 (CEB)

I was always taught as a young child that when you are in trouble you should pray. Obviously during my divorce prayer was in order. The problem was, sometimes I didn't feel like praying and other times I just didn't know what to pray about. There were times in which my emotions were so overwhelming, instead of praying I just cried out for help. I had so many questions about what types of prayers were appropriate during this difficult time. Of course in the beginning my prayers were selfish, they were all about me being able to make it through the anger, pain, fear, and shame I was experiencing. Soon I was able to pray for not only myself but others who were affected by our decision. My prayers included a variety of topics and questions including who, what, why, when, and how?

Who?

Who was I to pray for besides myself?

Me

I wanted to be selfish in my prayers because I was the one hurting. I wanted the pain to go away. I wanted the thoughts in my head to go away. I wanted to get some sleep at night. I wanted people to quit talking about me.

My-Ex

As much as I didn't want to, I had to pray for my ex. I was really afraid of him losing his job as pastor. If he lost his job, he wouldn't be able to pay child support, and where would we be? If nothing else, I knew what was important to him and did not want him to not be able to do what he loved more than anything else.

My Children

I have read many research studies on the effects of divorce on children and most of the information frightened me. Moving to a new home after relocating was going to be a challenge for my children. Having to change their schools especially after they had just adjusted to a new community could be frightening for them. Going back and forth from my house to their father's house every weekend wasn't fair. Divorce can lower a child's self-esteem. Children's school performance can be affected due to all the changes happening in children's lives. As a result of their frustrations, they can blame their parents and have ill feelings toward them.

Why?

During a few of my prayers, I felt the urge to ask God why I was going through this awful period. In divorce two, I surely asked why divorce was happening to me a second time. Why couldn't I stay married past seven years? Why could I not love my ex enough to stay married to him? Why did we move all the way to Kansas City and then go through this?

What?

At times I didn't know what to pray for. Should I pray that we be reconciled? I spent time asking God what His will in all of this was? Should I pray for a new job so I can better provide for my children? Should I focus on praying for forgiveness or the ability to forgive others? What was going to happen in my future? What would others think of me? What were my chances of finding love again? What good was going to come from all of this? Could God still use me in His service to be a blessing to others? I prayed that God could turn my mess into a message. What was I going to say?

Prayer Partners

I would encourage you to find a prayer partner who can pray with you before, during, and after the divorce process. However do not get someone who will just agree with everything you say. Ask the Lord to send someone who will not only pray with you but challenge you to stay in the presence of God. Someone who will seek God's guidance along with you will be most helpful in the long run. Maybe one of your best friends can fulfill this role or perhaps someone you have met in a divorce recovery group or single's ministry. Talk and pray with someone who has stayed in a marriage and also someone who has gone through divorce to get both perspectives. Ask God for discernment and to send the right person your way. Ask for not just a prayer partner but a prayer warrior who will storm heaven on your behalf.

Ask your Pastor or spiritual leader to pray with you and for you. Join an online support group for Christian women or find a spiritual mentor. There are numerous websites that offer spiritual guidance and support during this difficult time. You may even consider a professional divorce coach or counselor. Make sure you do your research and get references.

Study the Scriptures

The Bible has many scriptures to speak to your situation. Many I have included in this book, but there are many, many more to lead, guide, and direct you. Begin by finding scriptures on God's unconditional love. Locate God's promises and learn them by heart. Pray using scripture and watch God work miracles in your life.

Helpful Scriptures

You are my God and protector. Please answer my prayer. I was in terrible distress, but you set me free. Now have pity and listen as I pray. Psalm 4:1 (CEV)

LORD, God of my salvation, by day I cry out, even at night, before you— let my prayer reach you! Turn your ear to my outcry because my whole being is filled with distress; my life is at the very brink of hell. Psalms 88: 1-3 (CEB)

My eyes are tired of looking at my suffering. I've been calling out to you every day, LORD— I've had my hands outstretched to you! Psalm 88:9 (CEB)

I then turned my face to my Lord God, asking for an answer with prayer and pleading, and with fasting, mourning clothes, and ashes. Daniel 9:3 (CEB)

But I tell you to love your enemies and pray for anyone who mistreats you. Matthew 5:44 (CEV)

But Jesus would often go to some place where he could be alone and pray. Luke 5:16 (CEV)

Ask God to bless anyone who curses you, and pray for everyone who is cruel to you. Luke 6:28 (CEV)

Pray continually. 1 Thessalonians 5:17 (CEB)

CHAPTER 34
You are a Survivor

You were like a young wife, brokenhearted and crying because her husband had divorced her. But the LORD your God says, "I am taking you back! I rejected you for a while, but with love and tenderness I will embrace you again.
Isaiah 54:6 (CEV)

The Giant Fly

One cold Saturday morning in the month of January, we were experiencing an extremely cold winter. The night before, my current husband, Bobby, and I had gone out to dinner to celebrate my birthday. After returning home we had a movie marathon until the wee hours of the morning, so we were determined to sleep in. I typically get up at 5:00 a.m. during the week so on weekends I try to catch up on my sleep. The phone had already rung a couple of times, but we were being true to sleeping in and blocking out the world, so we didn't answer the phone. I was full of energy, but Bobby was still pretty tired. He happened to be lying in my arms so I didn't want to disturb him by jumping out of the bed. I wanted to get up and do some writing, but didn't want to be selfish. As I lay there, I began to pray and ask the Lord to help me to use my time wisely by speaking to me in the quietness of the morning.

I was trying to pray and be silent to listen to what the Lord wanted to tell me, when a giant fly flew by. I was extremely annoyed because I didn't expect to see anything flying around in our bedroom. Immediately I jumped up frightening Bobby out of his peaceful sleep. "Something's flying around in here," I screamed. Startled but not concerned, he asked me what it was.

"I only saw it once, but I think it was a fly, a giant fly," I said.

I suddenly remembered that it was around 14 degrees outside so it couldn't possibly be a fly. Before I knew it something big and black flew by us again. Bobby confirmed the flying pest was indeed a fly. My first question was, "How on earth could it be possible with it being so cold outside? Where did it come from and how did it manage to be so big?" I am not a scientist so I figured it was a miracle that it was still alive in the middle of winter. I imagined in my spirit that this fly had gone through something and had emerged victoriously to make its way to our warm bedroom. After we discussed the strangeness of having a large fly in our house in the middle of January, we tried to chase it down to kill it, but it had disappeared. We never saw the giant fly again.

Call me weird, but the fly came to my mind later in the day when I was spending quiet time in my office. I was curious, so I looked up information about flies. I learned the typical fruit fly thrives outdoors in warm temperatures and humidity, but as temperatures begin to drop in the fall, they eventually die. The fruit fly is one insect that cannot survive winter weather. I kept looking and discovered a fly called the cluster fly. Cluster flies, also known as attic flies, are usually larger than a common house fly. These flies breed and spend most of their time in the woods, migrating to buildings in the fall, looking for a warm place for the winter. They will usually find a spot warm around roof eaves or windows where the temperature is slightly warmer.

After reading all the exciting information about flies, I concluded that the cluster fly is a survivor. They may be slower than the fruit fly, but they manage to survive even the coldest of temperatures to emerge strong. The fruit fly can't handle the trial of going through the cold like the cluster fly can. Okay, so where am I going with the fly example? Regardless of the season the cluster fly is in, they learn to survive by doing what they have to do.

Surviving Your Season of Divorce

Divorce is for a season. Even if you are the one who desires to end the marriage, the season of divorce is difficult. I remember saying to myself, "If I survive this process, I will never get myself in this kind of mess again." Some mornings I didn't even want to get out of the bed and face the world, but I had to get up and be there for my children. I was determined the divorce wouldn't ruin me. I was going to be a survivor.

Perhaps you know someone who is a cancer survivor. My college best friend and sorority sister celebrates annually her freedom from breast cancer. She is thankful for her life and the grace God extended towards her. Recently my husband and I attended training to minister to cancer patients. They refer to their process as a journey. Those who have hope that they will make it through the journey fair better than those who have no hope.

Whatever you have faced during this difficult time, have the faith, hope, and belief that you are a survivor. Someday you will look back on this season in your life and be grateful for the grace of God which can bring you through. If I can survive being a two time divorcee, you can make it. Believe it or not, there are online divorce survivor groups. If online support groups interest you, search the internet for one that is right for you.

Remember, divorce is but for a season. Keep reminding yourself of how the seasons change. One of my least favorite times of the year is when daylight savings time ends in late October or early November and we fall back an hour. The change always means two things for me—the weather will be turning cold and everyday it will get dark around five o'clock in the evening. Because I get off work between 5:30 and 6:30 in the evening, I have to drive home in the dark. During the months of November and December, I long for the New Year when the days slowly begin to last longer. By the second week in January, the sun stays out a little longer. By the end of February, I no longer have to drive home in the dark. What helps me to get through November and December is knowing January and February are on their way and the darkness will no longer be an issue. My joy comes knowing that April is coming, when the time will go back to normal. I always remind myself "this too shall pass."

Regardless of what phase you are in, keep your faith and hope. Don't give up! Remember, "Weeping may endure for a night but joy comes in the morning" (Psalm 30:5). The night may seem long, but sooner or later, the sun is once again going to shine in your life. Just hold on and remember that you are a survivor!

Helpful Scriptures

God sent me before you to make sure you'd survive and to rescue your lives in this amazing way. Genesis 45:7 (CEB)

And you said: "Look here! The LORD our God has shown us his glory and greatness. We've heard his voice come out of the very fire itself. We've seen firsthand that God can speak to a human being and they can survive!
Deuteronomy 5:24 (CEB)

Let me give you some advice on how you and your son Solomon can survive this. 1 Kings 1:12 (CEB)

No, in all these things we are more than conquerors through him who loved us. Romans 8:37 (NIV)

And let us not be weary in well doing: for in due season we shall reap, if we faint not. Galatians 6:9 (KJV)

The LORD your God wins victory after victory and is always with you. He celebrates and sings because of you, and he will refresh your life with his love. Zephaniah 3:17 (CEV)

Don't worry about anything, but pray about everything. With thankful hearts offer up your prayers and requests to God. Then, because you belong to Christ Jesus, God will bless you with peace that no one can completely understand. And this peace will control the way you think and feel. Philippians 4:6-7 (CEV)

Chapter 35
Take Care of Yourself

You surely know that your body is a temple where the Holy Spirit lives. The Spirit is in you and is a gift from God. You are no longer your own. God paid a great price for you. So use your body to honor God. 1 Corinthians 6:19-20 (CEV)

I am an expert at taking care of everyone else. As I sit here putting the finishing touches on this book, I have a list of things I need to do for others. I have a scrapbook that needs to be completed from my daughter's graduation three years ago, I am helping out with the children's ministry at church, and I have some projects to finish for my boss before the end of the month. I have gone to work sick but stayed home when other members of my family were ill. I try to send encouraging texts or cards to others who are struggling with life's issues. I have a prayer list a mile long of people and situations I am praying for.

Every year, however, I make New Year's resolutions to take care of myself. Some of my typical promises to myself include: to eat organic, to work out at least 3-4 times a week, and to spend time in prayer and meditation daily. Usually within the first three weeks of the brand new year, I am back to my old habits of not doing things for myself and taking care of everyone else. Why do we do better at taking care of others than our own precious selves?

Every time you take a commercial airline flight, the attendant or the recorded message will give you instructions on how to apply an oxygen mask in case of a drop in cabin pressure. It goes something like this:

> *The cabin pressure is controlled for your comfort. However, should it change radically inflight, oxygen compartments will automatically open in the panel above your seat. Reach up and pull the mask to your face. This action will start the flow of oxygen. Place the mask over both your mouth and nose and secure with the elastic band as your Flight Attendant is demonstrating. Tighten by pulling on the ends of the elastic bands. Even though oxygen is flowing, the plastic bag may not inflate. If you are traveling with children, or are seated next to someone who needs assistance, place the mask on yourself first, then offer assistance. Continue using the mask until advised by a uniformed crew member to remove it.* (Airlineannouncements.com)

Please note the phrase "place the mask on yourself first, then offer assistance." The reason you are instructed to put your own mask on first is so you won't pass out. If you collapse due to a lack of oxygen you will be worthless to those around you. By not taking care of ourselves we are susceptible to additional emotional, psychological, spiritual, and physical problems including illness.

Protect Your Time

A good friend of mine by the name of Evelyn has a quote on her voicemail by Carl Sandburg: "Time is the coin of your life. It is the only coin you have, and only you can determine how it will be spent. Be careful lest you let other people spend it for you." Every time I leave her a voice mail, I am reminded of all the ways I allow others to steal my time. We all get the same amount of time, 24 hours a day or 168 hours a week. When I subtract the time I spend sleeping and working, I am left with 62 hours or almost eight hours a day to spend. How am I spending my leftover hours?

Who is stealing all of my time? For one week keep a time diary on the activities you participate in from the time you wake up in the morning until you go to bed at night. Who or what is stealing your time? Is your computer, tablet, or smart phone robbing you of your time? I love my iPhone and my iPad and my computer because they help me to be quite efficient. However, they are terrible time robbers just as the television can be. Do you find yourself vegging out in front of the television or scrolling your fingers through Facebook posts? I used to think texting was saving time, until I realized I could have a three minute telephone call and gain just as much information as I could with a text conversation that lasts for ten minutes. Whenever I text, I am usually multi-tasking which makes whatever I'm doing more complicated.

Learn to Say No

I used to pride myself on the ability to do it all. When my daughter was in the second grade, I somehow ended up being the homeroom mom. My daughter loved having me around to help with holiday parties and other activities. In talking with the other moms, I discovered I was one of the few that work full-time, as many of them were stay at home moms or only worked part-time. What was wrong with that picture? I had less time than everyone else did, but I sacrificed my own time to take care of the second grade class. I did the same for all of the sports teams my son participated in. Many times I was the taxi driver or the one responsible for bringing team snacks.

I get requests all the time including invitations to public events, parties, showers, fund raisers, invitations to volunteer my time and money, and personal requests from friends and family. I get approximately 100 emails a day, 25 to 30 texts a day, and four to five phone calls a day. If I view and respond to everything, I would have no life. Find a balance. I have learned to delete some apps and unsubscribe from some promotions as some companies attempt to bombard your life by sending out daily messages. I have learned to put my phone on silent and not look at it every time it makes a noise. I rarely answer my home phone now and limit who I give my cell phone number to. Learn to say no by not making yourself so accessible. Schedule a limited amount of time of day when you will return texts, emails, and phone calls. Program your phone to have a special ring for those you need to be in contact with.

Give Yourself a Break

The average employee who works eight hours a day is entitled to a 30 minute or one hour lunch break and two, 15 minute breaks. Wage and hour laws protect this right. I run around like the energizer bunny and feel guilty for taking a nap on Sunday afternoons. I had to learn how to give myself a break. A break may mean sitting down and sipping a hot cup of tea, taking a quick nap, taking a walk, curling up on the couch watching a movie, or reading a book. Reading a fiction book is a treat for me as I read two to three non-fiction books a week. Figure out what constitutes a break for you and do it.

Maybe you need a break from household chores. Your house does not have to be perfect all the time. After my daughter went off to school, I attempted a leave of absence from cooking. Yes, I still cooked from time to time but used my cooking time wisely. Instead of cooking every day, I made meals to last a couple of days or were simple and easy to make within 30 minutes. No more going to the grocery store several times a week and spending many hours in the kitchen for me. If you enjoy being in the kitchen, go for it, but for me not grocery shopping and cooking is a break.

When was the last time you went on vacation? Following my divorce, I splurged on myself and the kids and booked a trip to Cancun, Mexico. The kids and I had a great time, and I got some much needed sunshine and rest. Nothing is more peaceful for me than being near the ocean. Even though I live in the Midwest, I try to visit the coast at least once a year. Don't have the money to take an exotic trip? Try the newest trend and go on a staycation. I typically would not take off work to stay home, but I learned to appreciate the staycation concept. The real benefit was staying home when the kids had to go to school. If they were out of school, I ended up doing all the work. Plan something within the next 2-3 months for yourself. Set up a vacation account and save up enough money to take a trip you will enjoy. Pamper yourself. A manicure and pedicure is a great way to take a break.

Quiet Time

The world is so noisy. As I am sitting here typing, I can hear the air conditioner kicking on and off, the clothes dryer running, my neighbor cutting his yard, and traffic going down the street. I have Pandora playing on my iPad and I can hear the television on upstairs. Before long the telephone will ring or someone may ring the doorbell.

Not only is the world noisy, but our brains are noisy. I have many thoughts going through my mind right now. What am I going to eat for dinner? The weather is changing and I need to clean out my closet. I need to start making holiday plans. My blender is on its last leg and I need to get another one. Did my daughter get the job she applied for last week? I need to get to work early because I have a meeting or a special project I need to take care of. Have I paid all of my bills for the month? All of these thoughts went through my head in just a matter of minutes. Think of the many thoughts that go through our minds in a typical day.

To protect my sanity, I try to start my mornings out with some quiet time. I get up early to make sure the house is quiet. I go downstairs to my office before anyone else wakes up. My quiet time consists of reading the Bible, writing, praying, and meditating. I haven't quite mastered what I call real meditation, but I try to keep my mind from straying. Having 45 minutes to an hour of quiet time helps me to make it through the day. Don't have a quiet place to go to? Try the bathroom, it is one of the few places where it is acceptable to close the door and have peace and quiet. Not a morning person? Get your quiet time late in the evening or whatever time works best for you. Whatever you do, make your quiet time work for you.

> "We need quiet time to examine our lives openly and honestly - spending quiet time alone gives your mind an opportunity to renew itself and create order."
> Susan L. Taylor

Helpful Scriptures

I sleep and wake up refreshed because you, Lord, protect me. Psalm 3:5 (CEV)

A joyful heart helps healing, but a broken spirit dries up the bones. Proverbs 17:22 (CEB)

Many people were coming and going, so there was no time to eat. He said to the apostles, "Come by yourselves to a secluded place and rest for a while." Mark 6:31 (CEB)

Our health is restored, we feel young again, and we ask God to accept us. Then we joyfully worship God, and we are rewarded because we are innocent. Job 33:25-26 (CEV)

Your words and your deeds bring life to everyone, including me. Please make me healthy and strong again. Isaiah 38:16 (CEV)

For physical training is of some value, but godliness has value for all things, holding promise for both the present life and the life to come. 1 Timothy 4:8 (NIV)

Dear friend, I'm praying that all is well with you and that you enjoy good health in the same way that you prosper spiritually. 3 John 1:2 (CEB)

CHAPTER 36
Be a Blessing

When God's people are in need, be ready to help them.
Always be eager to practice hospitality.
Romans 12:13 (NLT)

The following scenario has happened to me on several occasions: I get a call from a woman who is unhappy in her marriage and wants to talk to me about how I made the decision to divorce my first husband. Usually the call comes from a woman who used to attend our church. When asked why she left the church in the first place, the most common response is because the pastor got a divorce. Remember divorce sometimes exposes vulnerabilities in other marriages. Funny, now they want my advice on how to leave their husbands.

The conversation begins by asking me about my experiences during my divorce process. Typical questions include: Who made the decision to divorce? How did you find a lawyer? What did you do first? After the questions, she will usually attempt to explain their current marital issue and that she is thinking about ending the marriage. A few have been involved in affairs and desire to leave their husband to be with another man. I listen to their marital concerns and problems and see the glimmer of hope in their eyes that the grass is greener on the other side.

I can tell by the look in their eyes that they are hoping I will suggest for them to leave their husbands. They are expecting me to tell them to walk away and their life will turn out great. They look at me, divorced with two children and now remarried with a wonderful husband and believe that it had to be easy because I am doing so great. In fact they often say, "Just look at you, you seem so happy, you look fantastic and everything has worked out so well for you."

I accept their compliments and am thankful to God that I look good in the public eye. At the same time I am disturbed in my spirit because I don't want people, especially women, looking at me thinking I have it all and that they could do better by ending their marriage. I do not want to be an influence that encourages others to end their marriage. I admit I have been extremely blessed but I do not think God wants me to be a poster child for why women should leave their husbands.

I gently instruct them that if they are involved in an affair to end the relationship immediately and deal with their marriage. The grass is not greener on the other side, but it's greener where you water it. I continue to explain the statistics for remarriage that 60-65 percent of remarriages fail especially when children are involved from previous relationships. Stepfamily life is no walk in the park and is sometimes a long difficult road to travel, even if you are fortunate enough to be in the 30 percent of couples who make it. I share my experiences being in a stepfamily. As much as possible I encourage them to stay with the husband they have and do everything they can to make the marriage work, including getting some counseling. Thankfully, so far, none of the women I have spoken with have gone on to get divorced.

Making Divorce Look Good

Is there such a thing as making divorce look too good? One afternoon I got a call from a young lady who is a member of our church. She wanted to let me know that her daughter had requested that she and her husband get a divorce. She was quite surprised by her daughter's request, as I was. Her daughter's rationale was that if her parents divorced, she could have two houses, two birthday parties, and two sets of Christmas gifts. Why? She wanted to have all of these things like my daughter.

The more I thought about our conversation, the more disturbed I became. Were other children envying my children and wanting to have a lifestyle like theirs? If they had asked my children, they would have told them that they were in no way living the dream life and would give up all the gifts and any other imagined perks to have their parents back together.

In no way do I ever want to glamourize divorce, but at the same time I want everyone to know that God is a merciful God that can help you through any situation. In my case, God did not allow me to physically look like I had been through divorce hell. On the outside I appeared fine. I am thankful to God for his mercy and grace. I do not want anyone to end their marriage based on my experiences. I make it very that God has taken my mess and turned it into a message.

On a Mission

I finally realize I have been called to help other women who are going through the divorce experience. It is my mission to encourage you that our God is a loving and forgiving God who will never leave you or forsake you during your time of trouble. I serve a God who can do anything but fail. Not only can he heal a broken marriage, but he can heal a broken heart and help you to move into the future He has prepared for you.

Keep your hearts and mind open as God may send others your way to hear your testimony. We have a responsibility to share God's goodness with others and to encourage others. You may be a listening ear and a support for another who is going through difficulties and struggles. Pray that God will send those who share similar experiences and that you can be a blessing to them. When sharing, reflect on your own experiences and discuss what you would have done differently knowing what you know now. At the same time, do not offer unsolicited advice and tell others what they should and should not do. Every situation is different. Pray before opening your mouth to speak. You don't want to cause someone else to stumble or make their situation worse. Lastly, practice discretion. Do not repeat another's personal business.

Also, remember there are tangible things that you can do to help someone in need. Offer to babysit for a couple while they go out on a date to work things out. Suggest a counselor or a couple they would benefit from speaking with. Gift a helpful book. Encourage him or her to attend a divorce recovery or support group. Most of all, be willing to be a listening ear, a shoulder to cry on, and an encourager that life will get better and what they are going through is just for a season.

Helpful Scriptures

But don't forget to help others and to share your possessions with them. This too is like offering a sacrifice that pleases God. Hebrews 13:16 (CEV)

Instead of each person watching out for their own good, watch out for what is better for others.
Philippians 2:4 (CEB)

Live creatively, friends. If someone falls into sin, forgivingly restore him, saving your critical comments for yourself. You might be needing forgiveness before the day's out. Stoop down and reach out to those who are oppressed. Share their burdens, and so complete Christ's law. If you think you are too good for that, you are badly deceived.
Galatians 6:1-3 (MSG)

Make your light shine, so that others will see the good that you do and will praise your Father in heaven.
Matthew 5:16 (CEV)

We who are strong have an obligation to bear with the failings of the weak, and not to please ourselves.
Romans 15:1 (ESV)

For God is not unjust so as to overlook your work and the love that you have shown for his name in serving the saints, as you still do. Hebrews 6:10 (ESB)

Love one another with brotherly affection. Outdo one another in showing honor. Romans 12:10 (ESV)

Chapter 37
Single and Satisfied

*I am not saying this because I am in need, for I have
learned to be content whatever the circumstances.
Philippians 4:11 (NIV)*

Occasionally, my single sister who has no children and I will compare our lives. She talks about how great it must be for me to have children and a husband. She speaks of the perceived benefits I have as a married woman with children. On the other hand, I will tell her how great life is for her because she is single and doesn't have to answer to anyone but herself. I mention the benefits of being single including having your own space, your own money, your own time, and your own life.

I remember my single days, I can say that I was truly single and satisfied, meaning I was happy being by myself and a relationship with a man was not required. I had fun hanging out with friends, having quiet time, and doing what I wanted to do. When my children were with their father every other weekend, I had some much deserved "me" time. As I noted before in a previous chapter I didn't necessarily have to be doing anything great, I found joy in going to the park or sitting at home in my favorite pajamas reading a book and staying locked up in the house for the entire weekend with the exception of going to church. Not being a pastor's wife, I really didn't have to go to church every Sunday but I did because I enjoyed church. At the time, we had an early morning service which was perfect for me.

Somehow for me, when I became content being single, men came out of nowhere. I was definitely not looking for a relationship. Many girlfriends commented that they had the perfect guy for me to meet. I declined several offers. As a member of the singles ministry at church one or two of the guys who were part of the group asked me out but I wasn't interested in a relationship at the time.

The Blessings of Being Single

In the Bible, the apostle Paul gives us the best view of the benefits of singleness. He shares with us that some people are called to be single, including himself. The personal life history of Paul is not fully discussed in the Bible but some say he was married at one time as his former job as a Sanhedrin required being married. Most commentaries suggest that his wife died. Paul refers to singleness as a gift because he was able to devote himself full time to the ministry he had been called to. Paul was one of the greatest Christians of all times because of his dedication to the gospel of Christ.

Read the seventh chapter of 1 Corinthians to understand Paul's views on being single. In my translation, he is simply saying, singleness is not for everybody but at the same time if you are single because of being a widow or divorced it may be to your benefit to stay that way until the Lord changes your situation either by giving you a spouse or giving you the gift to be able to appreciate and value being single.

Paul discusses the trouble that comes with being married, including having to get permission from your spouse to devote some special time to the Lord. He expresses that he wishes everyone could be like him but that not everybody can handle it. Paul is fully aware of the desires of the flesh, which is usually why some prefer not to be single. As I discussed in the temptation chapter, be careful of fleshly temptations. Don't let your bodily lusts get you in the wrong situation or lead you to sin. Paul is saying if you know you can't handle it, then pray for the Lord to send you someone rather than burning with desire which could lead to trouble.

What is your desire? Do you desire to be married, or can you be content being single? Following my divorce I still believed that marriage was good and desired and that I would someday remarry. However, at the time, I began to appreciate being single. As a parent there were many difficult moments, but I learned to build my network to help with the burdens of raising children alone. As a minister's wife I felt it was my job to make sure my husband was able to excel in the ministry. I seemed to be more concerned about him being able to do his job effectively than I was about my own relationship with God. Being single allowed me to serve him in a way I had not previously been able to.

Once I became single I found myself involved in several ministries at church where I was able to freely use the gifts God had bestowed on me. I loved working with the children, I loved teaching and fellowshipping with other Christian women, and I enjoyed having friends within the church family. Again, being a part of the single's ministry I was able to be a blessing to others and appreciated the fellowship and fun with other singles.

Lastly, peace and quiet was worth a million bucks. Not arguing all the time or not being miserable has benefits within itself. Yes, you have new worries but peace of mind is priceless.

Married to Jesus

I recently saw a woman wearing a shirt that read, *Married to Jesus.* Something tells me that's a new way of saying *single and satisfied.* Being married to Jesus means I know who I am in Christ and don't have to be married to be all I can be for God. I am dedicating my life to serving Him. He loves me for who I am and has promised that He will never leave me or forsake me. Take the time to reacquaint yourself with Jesus and experience the greatest love of all.

Helpful Scriptures

I wish all people were like me, but each has a particular gift from God: one has this gift, and another has that one. I'm telling those who are single and widows that it's good for them to stay single like me. But if they can't control themselves, they should get married, because it's better to marry than to burn with passion. 1 Corinthians 7:7-9 (CEB)

Now I will try to answer your other question. What about girls who are not yet married? Should they be permitted to do so? In answer to this question, I have no special command for them from the Lord. But the Lord in his kindness has given me wisdom that can be trusted, and I will be glad to tell you what I think. Here is the problem: We Christians are facing great dangers to our lives at present. In times like these I think it is best for a person to remain unmarried. Of course, if you already are married, don't separate because of this. But if you aren't, don't rush into it at this time. But if you men decide to go ahead anyway and get married now, it is all right; and if a girl gets married in times like these, it is no sin. However, marriage will bring extra problems that I wish you didn't have to face right now. The important thing to remember is that our remaining time is very short, and so are our opportunities for doing the Lord's work. For that reason those who have wives should stay as free as possible for the Lord; happiness or sadness or wealth should not keep anyone from doing God's work. 1 Corinthians 7:25-30 (TLB)

Chapter 38
Moving On

I know the plans I have in mind for you, declares the LORD; they are plans for peace, not disaster, to give you a future filled with hope. Jeremiah 29:11 (CEB)

Is it possible to turn a dying dream into a blessing? My dream was to be married and live happily ever after. Should I give up on my dream? Should I find a new dream? Where do I go from here? When we begin to think about the next chapter of our life, we are ready to move on. What does moving on entail? Where should you focus your energy? Here are some suggestions which may be helpful.

Get Social

While going through the divorce process, I felt like I was in hiding for at least six to eight months. The only places I went were to work, church, and to children's activities. I didn't eat out much or engage with a lot of people. Computer networking was not as popular with the exception of chat rooms. Now there is Facebook, Twitter, Instagram, and all kinds of electronic networking to keep you in touch with others. If you are into social networking, put a new profile picture of yourself out in cyberspace. Update your status to single and post something positive to let the world know you are doing fine as a single person. Make new friends, follow or like new people who make you smile. At the same time, do not overdo it and spend too much time on social media. Don't post your drama or everything going on in your life.

Join some type of club or group that interests you. What are your interests? Always wanted to be a part of a book club, a bowling league, or a car club? I joined the single's ministry at my church to network with other single Christians. Sports are a great way to get social. Join a softball or basketball team or a bowling league or take a cycling class or a Zumba class. Look on the internet and see what is in your area. Look at bulletin boards at local libraries and grocery stores. Pick up the local newspaper and see what's going on in your area. Don't have any interests? Take an online class or a day course at a local junior college on a topic you have always been curious about.

Invest in Your Career

Perhaps being married prevented you from having the career you always dreamed of. Take a look at your career goals and determine where you want to be in five years. Are you interested in a possible relocation or promotion? Look at the job board in your company and determine if there is a dream job you would like to pursue. Talk with your boss about taking on a new project or more responsibility. As I was going through my divorce, I realized I was going to need more money. I searched for and found a new job that gave me more financial security. With less marital stress I was better able to focus on my career.

While married I was presented with two opportunities to relocate but was unable to convince my spouse to move. After the divorce I was more flexible. I chose not to move because I wanted my children to be able to visit their father every other weekend. If you don't have children, relocating may not be a problem for you. Moving to a new location far away from your spouse or closer to your family may be just what the doctor ordered.

Keep Hope Alive

Your future is out there waiting for you. When you are ready, go for it. Not sure what your next move will be? Spend some time in contemplative prayer asking God's will for your life. Journal your thoughts about what you want to do. Research available options, put a plan together, and then execute your plan. Start with small changes and move on to bigger changes. Remain hopeful that the worst is behind you and life can only get better from here. Hope is the feeling that what is wanted can be had or that events will turn out for the best. Whatever you do, don't lose hope. Hope will help you to get out of the bed when you don't feel like it. Hope will convince you to make that call when you are fearful. Hope will keep you from falling apart on your difficult and frustrating days.

If you are lacking hope for your future, trust God to restore you. Read the promises written in the Bible pertaining to your future. Post scriptures on your mirrors or in your car. Memorize and recite scriptures that will encourage you throughout the day. Pray for hope and peace. Speak with someone who is encouraging. Listen to a motivational tape or sermon. Determine what activities give you hope. Keep your hope alive!

Dating

For some, moving on may mean a new relationship. Be careful not to get involved in a romantic relationship too soon. Wait at least a year. Two years is optimum. I have seen individuals jump out of one relationship and go immediately into another one. Not good. The last thing you want is to be in a rebound relationship. Take your time. Watch for others who will try to push you into the dating scene. Let friends know that you are not ready and that you will keep them posted when you are ready to meet someone. If and when you begin a new relationship, take it slow. Deal with any baggage you are carrying. Don't spend your energy talking about your former marriage and don't compare your date with your ex. Do not question your date about where the relationship is going too soon. Try to be yourself and have fun getting to know the other person. Write down a wish list of what you want in a potential mate. If you have been out of the dating scene for a while or never were in the dating scene, the rules may have changed. You may make some mistakes early on but learn from them quickly and keep moving forward.

Helpful Scriptures

We were saved in hope. If we see what we hope for, that isn't hope. Who hopes for what they already see?
Romans 8:24 (CEB)

There is still a vision for the appointed time; it testifies to the end; it does not deceive. If it delays, wait for it; for it is surely coming; it will not be late. Habakkuk 2:3 (CEB)

But it is just as the Scriptures say, "What God has planned for people who love him is more than eyes have seen or ears have heard. It has never even entered our minds!" 1 Corinthians 2:9 (CEV)

All you who wait for the LORD, be strong and let your heart take courage. Psalm 31:24 (CEB)

Unrelenting disappointment leaves you heartsick, but a sudden good break can turn life around.
Proverbs 13:12 (MSG)

Our Lord Jesus Christ himself and God our Father loved us and through grace gave us eternal comfort and a good hope. May he encourage your hearts and give you strength in every good thing you do or say.
2 Thessalonians 2:16-17 (CEB)

Then Joshua told the people to purify themselves. "For tomorrow," he said, "the Lord will do a great miracle."
Joshua 3:5 (TLB)

CHAPTER 39
Love and Remarriage

The priest answered them, "Go in peace, Your journey has the Lord's approval." Judges 19:6 (NIV)

While reading a book on divorce you may or may not be interested in ever finding love again or thinking about remarriage. During and after my divorces I did not even want to think about falling in love with someone else or getting married again. In fact I was irritated with my girlfriends who kept telling me I needed to meet someone new. I wasn't ready to think about my future in terms of being in another relationship.

We never know what God has planned for our life. Some of you may find love again and remarry. Some of you may stay single the rest of your lives. Some of you may end up reconciling with your spouse. I strongly suggest that you seek God's guidance and place your trust in Him to guide you in the right direction.

"Four years after my divorce, dating was the last thing on my mind. The divorce process had been difficult for my children and me, but life was going considerably well. We had made a new home for ourselves in the small community of Olathe, Kansas. The kids enjoyed their new schools and had adjusted well. I had a wonderful support system, including other single women I had met at church through the singles ministry. Every other weekend when my children went to visit their father, there was time to travel, catch up on work, hang out with girlfriends, be lazy, or do whatever I wanted to do" (Love, 2012 pg. 6).

You have just read the opening of chapter 1 of my first book, *One Plus One Equals Ten: A First Lady's Survival Guide for Stepmoms*. By now you know that after four years, I am remarried to the love of my life and have been for over twelve years now. We have a wonderful marriage despite the complications of adjusting to stepfamily life. We have defied the odds and are now experiencing a marriage much different than our prior marriages to former spouses. With Christ at the center of our marriage we are walking in agreement and trying to be a blessing to other couples and families.

Before I met my new husband, Bobby, I had gone on a few dates, but nothing serious. I hadn't met anyone I was really interested in. We started dating and quickly began to spend a lot of time together. I was frightened by how fast our relationship was moving. We were having a great time getting to know one another, yet I was afraid to share my heart with someone again. We spent hours talking about what had gone wrong in our first marriages and the mistakes we had made both as spouses and parents.

During our many conversations, we briefly talked about marriage. Even though both of us had failed at marriage with our former spouses, we still believed in marriage, meaning we both would consider marrying again. Within four months of dating, he proposed and we were married. We sought counseling from a pastor friend of Bobby's who also officiated our wedding ceremony.

Healing from divorce is possible with time. Sooner or later you may decide it is okay to find love and perhaps remarry. In the last chapter, I mentioned giving yourself plenty of time—at least two years after your divorce is final—before even considering a relationship. Don't ruin a possible relationship before it starts by jumping into something too soon. When the time is right, you may be ready to start a new chapter in your life. How do you know if you are ready to open your heart to love and a new relationship?

Joseph Kniskern, in his book *Making a New Vow* states, "To build a truly successful remarriage fully grounded in commitment, intimacy, and joy, we must know who we are in Christ. We also need to understand how our prior marriages affected us, and where we are in our personal recovery process, and how well prepared we are for remarriage." (Kniskern, 2003) If you are considering remarriage, I highly suggest reading his book. What I really appreciate about his book is that his wife, Cheryl, also provided valuable input on how to have a successful and happy remarriage.

Marriage and Family experts Les and Leslie Parrott in their book *Saving Your Marriage Before It Starts* cite seven predictors of a happy marriage:

>   Healthy expectations of marriage
>   A realistic concept of love
>   A positive attitude and outlook toward life
>   The ability to communicate their feelings
>   An understanding and acceptance of their gender differences
>   The ability to make decisions and settle arguments
>   A common spiritual foundation and goal

Lastly, if you are considering remarriage, seek counseling from your Pastor and/or a counselor. Attend a premarital conference. Every year, my husband and I deliver a special seminar on blended families at churches in our area. Knowing how to overcome the challenges of remarriage with children is crucial to make a remarriage work. Remember, remarriage with children is quite different from a first marriage when there are typically just two individuals starting a new life together. Often remarriage is bringing together two or more families with ingrained traditions and totally unique experiences. Based on our experience, I strongly suggest doing the work in advance with someone who is trained to help you answer key questions before you begin your journey.

Helpful Scriptures

And we know that all things work together for good to them that love God, to them who are the called according to his purpose. Romans 8:28 (KJV)

He who finds a wife finds what is good and receives favor from the Lord. Proverbs 18:22 (NIV)

There is no fear in love. But perfect love drives out fear, because fear has to do with punishment. The one who fears is not made perfect in love. I John 4:18 (NIV)

Love is patient, love is kind, it isn't jealous, it doesn't brag, it isn't arrogant, it isn't rude, it doesn't seek its own advantage, it isn't irritable, it doesn't keep a record of complaints, it isn't happy with injustice, but it is happy with the truth. Love puts up with all things, trusts in all things, hopes for all things, endures all things.
1 Corinthians 13:4-7 (CEB)

Many are the plans in a man's heart, but it is the Lord's purpose that prevails. Proverbs 19:21 (NIV)

There are three or four things I cannot understand: How eagles fly so high or snakes crawl on rocks, how ships sail the ocean or people fall in love. Proverbs 30:18-20 (CEV)

CHAPTER 40
Still Highly Favored

The woman left her water jar and ran back into town. She said to the people, "Come and see a man who told me everything I have ever done! Could he be the Messiah?"
John 4:28-29 CEV

As I prepare to bring this book to a close, let's take another look at the woman at the well and her encounter with Jesus. The woman at the well doesn't have a name, she is simply known as the Samaritan woman. We don't even know how old she is. We do know that she was important enough for Jesus to go out of his way to go to Samaria to encourage her. Typically women came to draw water in the morning to conduct their household duties. However, because of this woman's marital circumstances, she avoided the crowds. Most likely she did not feel comfortable being around other people which is why she came to the well to draw water at high noon.

Jesus was deliberate about having a conversation with her. When the conversation begins she is quick to try to put Jesus in check for even speaking to her. Societal rules did not allow men to talk to women especially if they were of a different race. Jesus breaks all boundaries by asking her for a drink of water. Thinking he was just being smart with her she held her own by asking him a few questions. Jesus in turn gives her a much better offer of living water. The living water sounds good to her because she would no longer have to come to the well. She was looking for relief from her current circumstances of being talked about by those in the community.

Jesus in a very kind manner brings up her marital situation. He does not condemn her, he just requests that she retrieve her husband. The woman has nothing to hide and admits that she has no husband. Jesus once again in a very mild manner informs her that he already knows her past in that she has had five husbands and her current situation of living with a man who is not her husband. Again he just states the facts and does not beat her over the head indicating what she has done wrong.

We don't know enough about the woman's history to know why she had been married five times. Was she married and divorced like myself? Or perhaps she was widowed five times and afraid to marry again after losing five husbands. Maybe she had been abused by one of her husbands or they just got up and left for no reason.

It really doesn't matter what her situation was before she had an encounter with Jesus, because meeting and talking with Jesus changes everything. Once the conversation is over and she realizes that she has been talking with the Messiah, she drops everything and is so excited she will tell anyone who will listen what Jesus has done for her. In fact her testimony is so strong that a whole town comes out to see Jesus based on what the woman has said.

Like the woman at the well, Jesus knows our past and our current situation. He knows that you are divorced, but he is not going to condemn you for it. Jesus loves you for who you are and wants to convince you that you are still in his favor. We no longer have to be ashamed because we are divorced, we are loved! Jesus doesn't want us to hide in shame and avoid living, he wants us to tell the world what he has done for us so that others can be blessed. Yes, I am divorced twice and now remarried and God's love for me has never changed.

From now on, live the highly favored life that God has planned for you. Let go of your past and move with confidence into your future—a future full of hope, love, and forgiveness. Trust God with your life and all your circumstances. Seek his guidance so you may know when and where you can share your divorce story. Wherever you are and whatever you do, always know that you may be divorced, but you are still highly favored!

Helpful Scriptures

When a ruler is happy and pleased with you, it's like refreshing rain, and you will live. Proverbs 16:15 (CEV)

I am your Creator. You were in my care even before you were born. Israel, don't be terrified! You are my chosen servant, my very favorite. Isaiah 44:2 (CEV)

And his master saw that the LORD was with him and that the LORD made all he did to prosper in his hand. So Joseph found favor in his sight, and served him. Then he made him overseer of his house, and all that he had he put under his authority. Genesis 39:3-4 (NKJV)

You have granted me life and favor, and Your care has preserved my spirit. Job 10:12 (NKJV)

For You, O LORD, will bless the righteous; with favor You will surround him as with a shield. Psalm 5:12 (NKJV)

For His anger is but for a moment, His favor is for life; weeping may endure for a night, but joy comes in the morning. Psalm 30:5 (NKJV)

The Lord make His face shine upon you, and be gracious to you; The Lord lift up His countenance upon you, and give you peace. Numbers 6:25-26 (NKJV)

May you have more and more grace and peace through the knowledge of God and Jesus our Lord. 2 Peter 1:2-3 (CEB)

CONCLUSION
Notes from the Author

Now unto him that is able to keep you from falling, and to present you faultless before the presence of his glory with exceeding joy. To the only wise God our Saviour, be glory and majesty, dominion and power, both now and ever. Amen. Jude 1:24-25 (KJV)

This book has forty chapters on purpose. The number 40 generally symbolizes a period of testing, trial, or probation. Think about Moses; he lived 40 years in Egypt and 40 years in the desert before God led the Israelites out of slavery. Think about Noah's ark and the flood and how it rained for 40 days. Hopefully what you have gained from reading this book is that divorce does not have to be the end of your story. Throughout this book I have attempted to reassure you that despite being divorced, you can live a rich, fulfilling, and blessed life. God is love and demonstrates his love by forgiving us and giving us hope for the future.

Hopefully, some of you started down the road towards divorce and changed your mind somewhere around chapter two or three. I am praying for those of you who will be lead to reconcile. May the resuming of your marriage be filled with love and laughter and the full reassurance that God will bless your determination to stay married. Remember, even if you have made it all the way to divorce court, reconciliation is still possible.

For those of you who were right in the middle of the divorce process while reading this book, I hope and pray I was able to help and encourage you during your darkest days. I hope you can accept the love and grace God so richly offers you despite what is going on in your life. On those days you didn't think you were going to make it, I pray you were encouraged by my words. I will continue to pray for your continued healing and the assurance that you are still blessed and highly favored of God.

For those of you who are now divorced and have walked around with this burden, I pray that you will accept God's gifts of grace and mercy. I hope you now realize that God is not mad at you and that he has a bright future planned for you. Some of you have now reached the single and satisfied stage in your life and I am happy for you. Continue to grow into the person God created you to be and remember that "with God, all things are possible."

If you have gone on to remarry, I pray that your new marriage is blessed. I hope this book has been helpful, and that you will use it as a resource. Share this book with others you know who are considering or have experienced divorce.

Several years ago, my husband and I developed a ministry called "Step with Love" to work with individuals, couples, and churches. We counsel couples, coach individuals going through changes in life and love, and help couples to un-complicate their blended families. As we continue to deliver premarital seminars designed to help families all over the country, our mission is to save families one step at a time and help them understand the demons that often destroy remarriages and blended families. We encourage you to visit our website at www.stepwithlove.org for additional tools and information.

It is my God given mission to use the skills I've learned from advance study and the writing of this book, to support others as a divorce coach and prayer partner. I am currently completing a doctorate program in Christian Counseling to further be a blessing to individuals contemplating or going through divorce. Please visit my website www.JaniceRLove.com for additional resources and encouragement. You may send confidential e-mails questions to jlove@stepwithlove.org.

Janice

Acknowledgements

To my husband – Rev. Dr. Bobby L. Love. Thank you for being the end of my complicated story. Thank you for reminding me again that with God all things are possible.

To my children – Austin and Addison. Thank you for supporting me as I tell our family story. Thank you for being proud of me despite my life choices.

To my bonus children – Brian, Bobby Jr., Jackie, Benjamin, Jasmine and Braxton. Thank you for still believing in marriage despite experiencing divorce in our family circle. Thank you for loving and accepting me.

To my spiritual prayer partners – Carol Dietzschold, Tina Richardson, Gina Washington, Connie Richardson, Deborah Jones, Deborah Donnell and Nette Robinson. Your daily prayers and encouraging scriptures kept me focused and encouraged.

To my siblings – Harriet Johnson, Jackie Weary, Gregorita Smith and Anthony Bowen. Thank you for being a part of my story and for putting up with my writing during family events.

To my proofreaders – Tasha Gatson, Luttra Lewis, Carol Dietzschold, Bettie Young and Beverly White. Thank you for being excited about proofreading my book and for your valuable insight.

To my editor – Michelle Chester. Thanks for your desire for perfection. By the way, I really do know what a comma is.

To author Ondrea Davis – Thank you for writing such a powerful forward in such a short period of time.

To my publisher, Dr. A'ndrea J. Wilson and Divine Garden Press – I am so blessed to have a thorough and supportive publisher. You are the best.

To my readers – Thank you for supporting and encouraging me by purchasing and sharing my books with others. Now unto him that is able to do exceedingly abundantly above all that we ask or think, according to the power that worketh is un (Ephesians 3:20 KJV)

Resources and References

Abramowitz, Alton. *When Divorce Is A New Year's Resolution,* The Huffington Post, Dec. 28, 2012.

Airline Announcements. Retrieved from http://airlineannouncement.com.

Barry, Michael. *The Forgiveness Project: The Startling Discovery of How to Overcome Cancer, Find Health, and Achieve Peace.* Grand Rapids, Michigan: Kregal Publications, 2011.

Ben-Zeen, Aaron. *Hating the One You Love, I Hate You but I Love You.* Psychology Today Blog. Retrieved from http://www.psychologytoday.com/blog/in-the-name-love/200804/hating-the-one-you-love-i-hate-you-i-love-you

Burgin, Debbie. *Steps to Regaining Self Esteem.* Retrieved from http://ezinearticles.com/?9-Steps-to-Regaining-Self-Esteem-After-Divorce&id=49025

Bishop, Brigid. *Hate is the Opposite of Love.* Retrieved from http://www.keen.com/CommunityServer/UserBlogPosts/Brigid_Bishop/Hate-is-NOT-the-Opposite-of-Love/119993.aspx

Borquez, Michelle, Connie Wetzell, Carla Sue Nelson, & Rosalind Spinks-Seay. *Live, Laugh, Love Again: A Christian Woman's Survival Guide to Divorce.* New York, New York: Warner Faith, 2006

Campbell, Bruce. *Counting Your Blessings: How Gratitude Improves Your Health.* The CFIDS & Fibromyalgia Self Help Program. Retrieved from www.cfidsselfhelp.org

Cancer Treatment Centers of America. Our Journey of Hope Cancer Leadership Training Manual. Rising Tide, 2013

Crooks, Richard D. *Finding God in the Seasons of Divorce: Volume 2: Spring and Summer Seasons of Renewal and Warmth.* Bloomington, Indiana: WestBow Press, 2013.

Diamond, Jed. *Surviving Male Menopause.* Naperville, Illinois: Sourcebooks, 2000.

Dobson, James and Shirley Dobson. *Night Light: A Devotional for Couples.* Sisters, Oregon: Multnomah Publishers, Inc. 2000.

Doskow, Emily. *Nolo's Essential Guide to Divorce 5th Edition.* NOLO Law for All. 2014

Donald Hughes. *The Divorce Reality.* Retrieved from TheatronMedia.com.

Deutschman, Alan. *Change or Die.* New York, New York: Regan Publishers, 2007

Edmonds, Molly. *How Anger Works.* 19 June 2008. HowStuffWorks.com. <http://science.howstuffworks.com/life/inside-the-mind/emotions/anger.htm (accessed December 28, 2014).

Ford, Debbie. *Spiritual Divorce: Divorce as a Catalyst for an Extraordinary Life.* San Francisco, California: Harper Collins, 2001.

Ford, Rachel. *Stress Management.* Retrieved from http://ezinearticles.com/?Stress-Management---When-Change-is-Stressful&id=3908154

Gallagher, Christine. *The Divorce Party Planner: How to Throw a Divorce or Breakup Party.* Retrieved from www.thediovorcepartyplanner.com

Holmes-Rahe Social Readjustment Rating Scale. *Journal of Psychosomatic Research*, (1967). Vol. 11, pp. 213-218.

Instone-Brewer, David. *Divorce and Remarriage in the Church: Biblical Solutions for Pastoral Realities.* Downers Grove, Illinois: IVP Books, 2003.

Kniskern, Joseph Warren. *Making a New Vow.* Nashville, Tennessee: Broadman & Holman Publishers, 2003.

Kniskern, Joseph Warren. *When the Vow Breaks: A Survival and Recovery Guide for Christians Facing Divorce.* Nashville, Tennessee: Broadman & Holman Publishers, 2008.

Love, Janice R. *One Plus One Equals Ten: A First Lady's Survival Guide for Stepmoms.* Soperton, Georgia: Divine Garden Press, 2012.

Martin, R. (2004). *Sense of humor and physical health: Theoretical issues, recent findings and future directions.* International Journal of Humor Research, 17, 1-19.

Masi, Kelly. *Stages of Grief for Divorce.* Retrieved http://www.ehow.com/list_7621341_stages-grief-divorce.html#ixzz2s6NCyLaj (accessed December 30, 2014).

McGee, J. Vernon. *Marriage Divorce.* Nashville, Tennessee: Thomas Nelson Publishers, 1998.

Moore, Chanté. *Will I Marry Me?* Chanté Moore CM7 Entertainment, 2014.

Okawa, Ryuho. *10 Principles of Universal Wisdom.* Delhi, India: Jaico Publishing, 2008.

Omartian, Stormie. *Praying Through the Deeper Issues of Marriage.* Eugene, Oregon: Harvest House Publishers, 2007.

Parrott, Les and Leslie Parrott. *Saving Your Marriage Before It Starts.* Grand Rapids, Michigan: Zondervan, 2001.

Petherbridge, Laura. *When I Do Becomes I Don't: Practical Steps for Healing During Separation & Divorce.* Colorado Springs, Colorado: David C. Cook, 2008.

Sbarra, David A., Robert E. Emery, Christopher R. Beam, & Baily L. Ocker. *Marital Dissolution and Major Depression in Midlife: A Propensity Score Analysis.* Clinical Psychological Science May 2014 vol. 2 no. 3 249-257.

Salholz, Eloise. *"Too Late for Prince Charming?"* Newsweek. 2 June 1986.

Stevenson, Betsey and Wolfers, Justin. *Bargaining in the Shadow of the Law: Divorce Laws and Family Distress.* The Quarterly Journal of Economics (2006) 121 (1): 267-288.

The Barna Group, Ltd. *New Marriage and Divorce Statistics Released.* Retrieved from https://www.barna.org/barna-update/article/15-familykids/42-new-marriage-and-divorce-statistics-released#.UnjdOL7nZZc

Tutu, Desmond & Tutu, Mpho. *The Book of Forgiving: The Fourfold path for Healing Ourselves & Our World (e-book).* San Francisco, California: Harper One, 2014.

U.S. National Center for Health Statistics. *National Vital Statistics Reports (NVSR) Births, Marriages, Divorces, and Deaths: Provisional Data for 2009*, Vol. 58, No. 25, August 2010, and prior reports.

WebMD. *Depression.* Retrieved from http://www.webmd.com/depression/guide/untreated-depression-effects?

Weintraub, Pamela with Stephen R. Clark. *Christian Family Guide to Surviving Divorce.* Indianapolis, Indiana: Alpha Books, 2003.

About the Author

Janice R. Love is the author of *One Plus One Equals Ten: A First Lady's Survival Guide for Stepmoms*. She holds a Master's in Psychology and in a doctoral candidate in Christian Counseling. Janice is a certified stepmom coach, divorce coach, and prayer partner. She lives in Kansas where she is married to ministry partner and Pastor, Dr. Bobby. Love, Sr., and is at work on her next book.

Check out Janice's Bestselling Inspirational Book
ONE PLUS ONE EQUALS TEN
A FIRST LADY'S SURVIVAL GUIDE FOR STEPMOMS

AVAILABLE NOW IN PAPERBACK AND E-BOOK
WWW.DIVINEGARDENPRESS.COM
WWW.JANICERLOVE.COM

www.ingramcontent.com/pod-product-compliance
Lightning Source LLC
Chambersburg PA
CBHW071306110426
42743CB00042B/1188